Ethnicity and Aboriginality:
Case Studies in Ethnonationalism

Ethnonationalism is a phenomenon of great importance in many parts of the world today. In this collection of papers eight distinguished anthropologists focus on Canadian and international case studies to show ethnonational claims of cultural groups have been expressed and developed in specific historical and political situations. From observations of Quebec, to problems of the Australian Aborigines, Malay identity, the Avalogoli in Western Kenya, and ethnic cultures in Nigeria, the essays reflect the complexity of the claims and aspirations of different groups. Some deal with intractable demands for sovereignty, others with solutions that attempt to achieve a level of autonomy and recognition short of sovereignty.

The intellectual history of the right of self-determination is little more than 200 years old. It is only since that time that the ideal of popular sovereignty by any group that sees itself as a people became an accepted view. These writers have used a paper by Walker Connor, 'The Politics of Ethnonationalism,' as a foil against which to develop their own theses. Connor argues that claims to self-determination based on ethnic identity present problems to all but a few states, and since these claims are unlikely to be satisfied, ethnonationalism is disruptive of political order. The contributors to this volume do not accept his negative conclusions, although they share a sense that secession and division are less worthy outcomes than pluralist structures. Since ethnonationalism will continue to be a political issue for some time, these papers form a significant base for future political debate.

MICHAEL LEVIN is a member of the Department of Anthropology, University of Toronto.

Ethnicity and Aboriginality:
Case Studies in Ethnonationalism

Edited by Michael D. Levin

UNIVERSITY OF TORONTO PRESS
Toronto   Buffalo   London

© University of Toronto Press Incorporated 1993
Toronto Buffalo London
Printed in Canada

ISBN 0-8020-2918-3 (cloth)
ISBN 0-8020-7423-5 (paper)

Printed on acid-free paper

Canadian Cataloguing in Publication Data

Main entry under title:

Ethnicity and aboriginality : case studies in ethnonationalism

Contributions to a symposium titled Ethnonationalism:
Canadian and International Perspectives held in
December 1990 at New College, University of Toronto.
ISBN 0-8020-2918-3 (bound)
ISBN 0-8020-7423-5 (pbk.)

1. Ethnicity – Congresses. 2. Indigenous people –
Congresses. 3. Self-determination, National –
Congresses. 4. Nationalism – Congresses. I. Levin,
Michael D., 1942– .

GN495.6.E85 1993   305.8   C93-093973-5

In memorian:

Sally Weaver
1940–1993

Contents

Preface

The papers in this volume were contributions to a symposium titled 'Ethnonationalism: Canadian and International Perspectives' held in December 1990 at New College, University of Toronto. In all, eleven papers were read at the symposium and of these seven are published here. An eighth, by Judith Nagata, who was a principal discussant, has been added. The inclusion of papers in this collection depended solely on whether the paper addressed the central theme of the symposium.

The term 'ethnonationalism' was chosen as the theme of the symposium to focus participants' thinking on what is called in the Introduction, the strong version, that every people has a right to be a nation, that is, to its own state and the implications of this notion. The necessity, naturalness, and inevitability of the creation of a state by each ethnonational movement was suggested as the focus of questions to be raised by participants. The point of departure was a 1973 paper by Walker Connor entitled 'The Politics of Ethnonationalism' (published in the *Journal of International Affairs* 27(1): 1–21). After giving a lengthy list of countries whose politics involve ethnonational movements, Connor notes that only fourteen (since 1991, with the unification of Germany, only thirteen) are culturally homogeneous and without such movements. Although the symposium was not intended as a critique or discussion of Connor as such, since most participants began with Connor before departing significantly from his views, his paper served as a point of reference for and a stimulus to discussion.

The conceptual debate, finding labels for forms of cultural differentiation, is a continuing one. 'Ethnonationalism' came under early criticism for its linking of 'ethnos' with 'nation.' This association was thought to be too strong. The organizers of the symposium had hoped for that kind of response. A number of terms have been proposed to embrace both 'ethnic group' and 'aboriginal' or, in Canada, 'First Nations.' During the conference the term 'ethnocultural' was suggested. Ethnocultural seemed to some to emphasize the link between the people and culture as the basis of group politics. Some have argued for ethnicity as a characteristic of all human groups, a universal definition independent of minority or majority status (Glazer and Moynihan 1975, Introduction, p. 4), but the term 'ethnic' has tended to be identified with immigrants. Indigenous, autochthonous, or aboriginal peoples wish to assert a claim of priority especially in the New World, Australia, and New Zealand. Ethnic merges them with later immigrants. Ethnocultural may resolve some of these difficulties, but it does not seem to carry the political emphasis desired (see Conclusions).

The capitalization of certain words, names designating historical and ethnic status, has proved to be controversial. Most publishers prefer minimal use of initial capitals whenever possible. Guides to writing are not so unequivocal, suggesting that when words are used in a technical sense, when attributes are used as proper names, and when referring to nationalities and their languages, races, and tribes, initial capitalization is appropriate. The publisher of the *Canadian Native Law Reporter*, at the end of 1991, changed its editorial policy: 'The Native Law Centre has adopted the policy of capitalizing the words "Aboriginal," "Native," and "Indigenous" in all instances, except in quotations where the original spelling is retained' (page i).

The practice of contributors to this book has led to the following compromise on capitalization. In, and in regard to, Australia, it is clear that Aborigine and Aboriginal are in the class of proper names and ought to be capitalized. In Canada, the name Indian is coming to be used less because it was from the beginning a misnomer, but has not been fully replaced as has Eskimo by Inuit. Native is the most widely used term to embrace Indians, Inuit, and Métis. In this book, Native is therefore capitalized. Aboriginal is capitalized in reference to Australia, but not Canada. Indigenous, rarely used in the sense of a proper name when the papers were written, is also not capitalized.

I trust that readers of this book realize that I and the other contributors know that the forms of names connote important emotional and political dimensions of recognition, and I trust also that readers will recognize our commitment to the realization of the value of self-determination, and will therefore accept the editorial compromise achieved here. The need for consistency in form in this work is in no way intended to diminish the validity of, or respect for, any people's aspirations of self-determination.

REFERENCE

Glazer, Nathan, and Daniel P. Moynihan (eds.). 1975. *Ethnicity: Theory and Experience.* Cambridge: Harvard University Press

Acknowledgments

For their assistance in organizing the symposium I should like to thank Michael Asch and Leslie Jermyn.

Financial and other material support were given by the Social Science Research Council of Canada; Samuel and Saydie Bronfman Foundation; Sonya Bata; Dr H. McLaughlin, Science Centre of Ontario; at the University of Toronto: the President and Provost; Snider Lecture Fund, Faculty of Arts and Science; Principal, New College; Chair, Department of Anthropology; the Robert F. Harney Professorship of Ethnic, Immigration, and Pluralism Studies; Canadian Studies, University College.

For assistance in the organization of the symposium special thanks are due, at New College, to Ruth Reiffenstein, Lyn Michisor, and Paul Ellul, and to graduate students of the Department of Anthropology, Rosalind Farber, Leslie Jermyn, and Meg Sellors.

In the symposium itself, participants whose papers do not appear here, and discussants, without whose detachment and commentary we would have been left without a sense of the unity of the ideas presented and their relevance and value, must also be recognized, including Rafiuddin Ahmed, Cornell University; Alain Bissonette, Conseil des Atikamekw et des Montagnais, Quebec; Noel Dyck, Simon Fraser University; Harvey Feit, McMaster University; Gerald Gold, York University; Dipankar Gupta,[1] Jawaharlal Nehru University, Delhi, India; Toby Morantz, McGill University; J.E.

Chamberlin, W.W. Isajiw, and K. Sieciechowicz, University of Toronto.

NOTE

1 Dr Gupta has published a version of his paper, 'Ethnic Imagos and Their Correlative Spaces: An Essay on Some Aspects of Sikh Identity and Perception in Contemporary Punjab' in *Contributions to Indian Sociology* (n.s.) 26, 2 (1992): 223–44.

Ethnicity and Aboriginality

If the ideal expression of self-determination is to be found in the strong sense of ethnonationalism – the creation of new states out of existing states – the goals are clear, but the subsequent problems, secessions, and conflicts over assets and sovereignty are likely to seem interminable, if not beyond resolution. Recognition of the practical problems is not likely to solve them, since the aspirations for unity of the state and those for secession to create a new state both draw ideological sustenance from the same ideals of self-determination and sovereignty. There is some irony in the absoluteness of the solution; the state, legitimized by an open, tolerant, relativist ideology of self-determination weakens itself in acknowledging the same rights for peoples within its boundaries.

Acceptance of the right to self-determination – the weak sense of ethnonationalism – also presents problems, since it leaves unanswered the question of what forms of institutional recognition can meet the aspirations of 'people' for autonomy. This right, widely proclaimed, and valued, is no less difficult to realize. The opposition between the generality of self-determination and the absolute singularity of ethnonationalism generates a conservatism in solutions. New political forms which offer autonomy but do not offer sovereignty are difficult to imagine. Furthermore, any new solution bears the burden of achieving acceptance without a history to give it legitimacy. The reduction of the idea of ethnonationalism to general solutions and universal values makes any innovation suspect. On closer examination, however, some claims to nationhood are expressed in terms of the strong sense of ethnonationalism, but recognize alternative possibilities in their demands for new institutional arrangements. Examples in Canada are the concepts of 'sovereignty–association' for Quebec and 'self-government' for Canadian First Nations peoples.

The justifications of ethnonationalism – identity and aspiration – are as strongly formed as the concept of self-determination. Identity and aspiration seem to have a 'naturalness in origin' that makes them difficult to reject. To define a 'people' requires a recognition of distinctiveness that attaches uniquely to a group. Ethnic identity is the most widely used basis for legitimacy not only for minorities, but also for majority groups sharing a common culture. An ethnic group that is a majority may attempt to imprint its culture on the state.

Aboriginality is a more refined claim to distinctiveness based on historical experience. It emphasizes status as the original occupants of a place, adding depth to the idea of cultural differences. The use of aboriginality as a basis for ethnonational claims does not have the universalism of ethnic claims and is restricted to those places 'discovered' by Europeans after 1492 in both the Old and New Worlds. As well as a basis for ethnonational claims, it is also a claim against immigrant ethnic groups.[1]

The form of the claim for status as a people and the urgency arising out of self-awareness often depend on a history that links identity with events threatening that identity. A claim may embody an 'ethnodrama,' a history of denial and victimization, sometimes genocide, as do histories of the Jews, Armenians, and New World native peoples, which justifies nationalism and a state as the only means of survival. More moderate threats, not to physical survival, but to culture and language, as in the case of Quebec, are also used to justify secession. The logic of ethnonationalism in these instances is unassailable.

The papers in this book reflect the complexity of the claims and aspirations of different groups and the varying forms of expression of these ideals. Some papers deal with the intractable demand for sovereignty, others with solutions being advocated or attempted that achieve some level of autonomy and recognition short of sovereignty. The protection and nurturing of culture is the core of some demands, but political separation the only possibility in others.

In conceiving of the conference 'Ethnonationalism: Canadian and International Perspectives' the organizers proposed that the contributors use the strong version of ethnonationalism as outlined in Walker Connor's paper 'The Politics of Ethnonationalism' (Connor 1973) as a foil against which to develop their analyses of ethnonational issues. Connor argues that claims to self-determination based on ethnic identity present problems in all but a few states, and since these claims are unlikely to be satisfied, ethnonationalism is disruptive of political order. His emphasis on the problematic aspects of ethnonationalism and his pessimistic conclusion would give little comfort to aspirants to self-determination, but Connor's paper does make clear the modernity of ethnonationalism and the intellectual history of its supporting ideas.

Although the papers in the present volume do not follow Connor's argument closely, they were written and discussed in the context of the 'problematic' perspective that he puts forward. Because 'The Politics of Ethnonationalism' lent so much to the discussion it is worth giving Connor's views in some detail.

Walker Connor describes the central dilemma of ethnonational politics as follows: 'In a world consisting of thousands of distinct ethnic groups and only some one hundred and thirty-five states, the revolutionary potential inherent in self-determination is quite apparent.' This is what might be termed the crude practical dilemma of ethnonational politics: how to match each ethnic group with its own state. From this perspective ethnonational aspirations seem natural and timeless, but Connor's discussion of the phenomenon shows that this is not the case. Ethnonationalism is a relatively new political force and it derives its political and moral legitimacy from ideas of the late eighteenth and early nineteenth centuries, in particular what he calls 'the principle of national self-determination.' Despite its status as an almost universally accepted, or self-evident, truth, national self-determination is poorly reflected in the reality of the world's states, all but thirteen of which contain a significant minority population.[2] As Connor emphasizes, however, the lack of correspondence between the ideal and reality, that is the apparent failure to actualize the principle, 'should not be taken as an index of either the principle's popular appeal or of its political impact to date' (Connor 1973: 1). Finally, the continuing force and form of the principle of national self-determination and this striking contrast of the reality in most states to it, is the source of 'serious ethnopolitical discord' in many states (1973: 11). Despite the various government responses to 'the threat of ethnonationalism' none has found 'a workable solution' (1973: 18–19).

The intellectual history of the right of self-determination is rather short, little more than 200 years, yet ethnic groups have existed for much longer (Smith 1986). Cultural differences, language, and custom, the distinguishing characteristics of ethnic groups, do not create nations. Self-consciousness and awareness of other groups is necessary to make an ethnic group a nation. Ethnic groups may be defined by others, but it is only when members become aware of their own uniqueness that a group moves from being an ethnic group to becoming a nation. Self-awareness alone, however, is not sufficient, historically, for the idea of self-determination to gain its political potential. It is only in an era in which the ideal of popular sovereignty is widely accepted that any group that views itself as a people 'is apt to view a right to create its own state as self-evident and incontestable' (Connor 1973: 5).

The power of the ideas of popular sovereignty and national self-determination is evident in recent world history. Their universal appeal allows them to be harnessed to popular causes, and their use widens their dissemination. It is common for the governments of states, for example, both India and Pakistan, that achieved their independence from colonial rule on the basis of slogans about the people and self-determination, to attempt to deny these legitimizing ideas to ethnonational movements within their borders. The universality of the ideas, however, does not respect group boundaries. Indeed, these ideas could be said to create boundaries by enhancing awareness of distinctiveness.

Walker Connor also examines the practical implications of aspirations for self-determination of ethnic groups and finds, not surprisingly, insurmountable problems in matching territory and ethnicity. He is equally pessimistic about government programs designed to accommodate ethnonationalism, finding most to be ethnically unacceptable or unworkable (1973: 19). He concludes with a pessimistic prediction about the future of ethnonationalism that has proved to be exaggerated only in its understatement: 'The contagion of self-determination of nations' is far from spent as a political force' (1973: 21). Two decades since the publication of Connor's paper, violence, war, and murder along ethnic lines, in the states of the former Soviet Union, Yugoslavia, India, and Burma, support the tragic accuracy of his conclusion.

The papers in the present volume do not subscribe to Connor's narrow framework for self-determination, nor do they accept his strongly negative conclusions. In tone, they share the sense that secession and division are less worthy outcomes than pluralist structures that allow for cultural autonomy of minority and majority groups. As a set of case studies, they illustrate the difficulties in satisfying ethnonational demands. Canada, Malaysia, and Nigeria offer a range of alternatives. Since ethnonationalism will most certainly continue to be a political issue, the value of these studies lies in the understanding gained from the comparisons of the possibilities for accommodating cultural pluralism.

NOTES

1 It should be noted that, ironically, the first nationalist claims were not made on a linguistic or cultural basis, but on a purely political basis of popular resentment of imperial rule. These were made in South America against Spain, in the late eighteenth century (Anderson 1991).
2 Connor notes fourteen states which do not contain significant minorities and of those seven characterized by irredentist situations with the dominant ethnic group extending beyond the state's borders. One pair in the

irredentist category was the Germanies, whose unification reduces the number of states to thirteen.

REFERENCES

Anderson, Benedict. 1991. *Imagined Communities: Reflections on the Origins and Spread of Nationalism*, 2nd ed. London: Verso
Connor, Walker. 1973. 'The Politics of Ethnonationalism.' *Journal of International Affairs* 27(1): 1–21
Smith, Anthony D. 1986. *The Ethnic Origins of Nations*. Oxford: Basil Blackwell

CHAPTER 1

Ethnonationalism, Aboriginal Identities, and the Law

Patrick Macklem

In an influential article entitled 'The Politics of Ethnonationalism,' Walker Connor notes a growing tendency among individuals and groups to link political legitimacy with ethnic identity. The principle of national self-determination, premised upon the acceptance of such a linkage, is the legal and political counterpart to what Connor coins ethnonationalism: namely, the belief that 'political institutions and borders [ought] to conform with the best interests of the ethnic group' (Connor 1973: 2). In Connor's view, two elements set the stage for the introduction of ethnonationalism to the ideological politics of a contemporary state. The first is a 'self-awareness of the existence of the ethnic group in question,' which in turn presupposes an awareness of other groups (1973: 3). The sense of being different requires a referent, a 'them'; being different, in other words, requires the construction of an other. The second element responsible for the emergence of ethnonationalism is the success of the notion of popular sovereignty. When wedded to claims of ethnic or cultural difference, the idea that political legitimacy resides in the people provides powerful support to ethnonationalist claims for greater autonomy.

Walker Connor's views provide valuable insight into Native peoples' demands for greater control over their individual and collective identities and a restructuring of the Canadian state to accommodate indigenous difference. Such demands are premised on notions of cultural difference and the belief that aboriginal peoples possess unique historical and cultural identities worthy of protection from the assimilative tendencies of the dominant, colonizing 'other.' Moreover, First Nations have asserted the right of self-determination in international contexts and the right of self-government in domestic contexts; both assertions obtain their persuasive power in part from notions of popular sovereignty. While 'ethnonationalism' may not be an entirely apt term to describe a set of beliefs geared toward the liberation of indigenous peoples from the oppressive weight of colonial practice, Connor's insights help to explain the new-found currency to Native peoples' claims for greater control over their individual and collective identities.

What interests me, however, is not so much the explanatory power of Connor's analysis in relation to the genesis and development of First Nations demands for greater political autonomy, but instead how Connor characterizes state responses to ethnonationalist demands. In his words, 'there is a seemingly universal tendency on the part of governmental leaders to make all decisions subject to the implicit or explicit presumption that the political integrity of the sovereign territory – no matter how acquired and no matter how diverse the people who occupy it – is simply incontestable' (1973: 12). Ethnonationalist claims are resisted by state authorities through and by a form of decision-making that precludes from serious discussion the very thing that ethnonationalist claims call into question: the political integrity of the sovereign territory. According to Connor, 'the presumption that the state is a *given* and must not be compromised therefore causes governments to resist, if need be with force, any attempt to dismember the state in the name of self-determination' (1973: 12).

This essay attempts to track how the aspiration of Native people to have greater control over their individual and collective identities has been received or dealt with by the Canadian legal system. It seeks to demonstrate that Connor's description of state responses to ethnonationalist claims is an especially apposite characterization of the law's response to Native peoples' aspirations for greater control over their individual and collective identities. I hope to determine the way in which the Canadian legal system has resisted ethnonationalist claims by its indigenous population. If ethnonationalism requires a referent, the construction of an other, the resistance that ethnonationalism engenders in political and legal structures can also be explained by reference to the construction of an other. Turning Walker Connor's point on its head, the same type of consciousness that drives ethnonationalism also underpins and supports the political and legal system against which ethnonationalism is directed.

More specifically, First Nations claims to autonomy are made in and against a political and legal system that historically saw human relations from the vantage point of the legal imagination of the colonizing power, a system that demanded that political and legal institutions and borders conform to the best interests of the colonizing power and not threaten basic organizing categories of the colonial legal imagination. The incontestability of the integrity of Canadian sovereign authority is established and maintained in legal discourse by a rhetoric of similarity and difference. The law has constructed Native people as different when to acknowledge their similarities would threaten basic organizing categories of the Anglo-Canadian legal imagination, but it simultaneously has viewed Native people as similar to non-Native people when to acknowledge difference would threaten basic legal categories of the Anglo-Canadian legal imagination. This interplay of similarity and difference constitutes the rhetoric of justification that has legitimated the imposition of non-Native legal norms onto Native society by the judiciary. The imposition of Anglo-Canadian legal norms onto Native reality has been critical to the establishment and maintenance of legal relationships of dependence between Native peoples and the Canadian state.

First formulated in the context of gender, the recognition that acknowledgment *and* denial of difference can perpetuate inequality has been referred to by Martha Minow as 'the dilemma of difference' (Minow 1987). I believe a similar interpretive dilemma exists with respect to First Nations and the law. The critical question is not whether differences and similarities exist, for they surely do, but instead is the use to which similarities and differences are put by the law. Does the legal identification of similarities and differences work to perpetuate hierarchical relationships between races or cultures, or does it work to facilitate the establishment of institutional arrangements wherein Native people themselves can participate in defining their individual and collective identities and their similarities and differences from non-Native people? The latter route would acknowledge that aboriginal identities are not innate and immutable, discoverable through legal inquiry, but rather negotiated and constructed through the interplay of self-knowledge and communal understandings (Clifford 1988; Minow 1991).

Instead of facilitating the establishment of legal spaces in which aboriginal identities could be negotiated and constructed by First

Nations themselves, the law has arrogated to itself the power of naming aboriginal identity and, in so doing, has profoundly affected the processes by which individual and collective aboriginal identities are constructed and maintained. The law's embrace and denial of difference has not only justified the establishment and maintenance of legal relations of hierarchy, but also has had the effect of constructing a legal aboriginal identity, a Native 'other' in the eyes of the law. Legal aboriginal identity in turn has shaped the individual and collective identities of aboriginal people. Individual and collective aboriginal self-understandings have been shaped and constituted in part by a complex form of resistance and acceptance of aspects of an aboriginal identity that the law holds out to First Nations as their own. The drive for self-government, the Native equivalent of an ethnonationalist impulse, is an attempt to seize control from non-Native authorities over the process by which aboriginal identities are constructed.

A logic of racism permeates the rhetoric of justification that legitimates Canadian legal practice. This is not to suggest that judicial decision-makers intentionally view Native people as inferior to non-Native people. Many decisions have been rendered which explicitly seek to assist First Nations in their dealings with the Canadian state. Nor is it to suggest that similarities and differences do not exist between Native people and non-Native people. The law's logic of justification, however, identifies and uses similarities and differences between Native and non-Native people to perpetuate hierarchical relationships between First Nations and the Canadian state. Relations of power are constructed and maintained by the identification of racial and/or cultural difference. The use to which similarity and difference are put can be said to be racist to the extent that it legitimates racial or cultural inequalities between Native and non-Native people. Such is the case with Canadian law and the continued imposition of non-Native categories of legal understanding onto Native reality.

Two legal categories that have been imposed onto Native reality by the Canadian judiciary are Canadian sovereignty and private property. Each involves the creation and maintenance of a specifically legal relationship of dependence between First Nations and the Canadian state. Reliance on Native difference has established a sovereign/subject relationship between the Canadian state and First Nations. Reliance on Native similarity has rendered aboriginal relations to ancestral lands subject to the goodwill of the Crown. Both areas frustrate rather than facilitate the creation of legal spaces in which Native people can gain greater control over their individual and collective identities. Each is addressed in turn.

CANADIAN SOVEREIGNTY

When the North American continent was settled by European nations, there obviously were indigenous inhabitants who had been living there for centuries with their own ways of social, economic, and political organization (McMillan 1988). How is it that the settling nations were able to make claims of sovereignty over these people, claims that form the historical backdrop to contemporary assertions of Canadian sovereignty over Canada's First Nations? In the debates surrounding Confederation, there was no discussion whatsoever about the propriety of asserting Canadian sovereignty over Canada's indigenous population. Sovereignty was assumed, and its assumption is basic to the Canadian legal imagination. Aboriginal peoples in Canada currently are imagined in law to be Canadian subjects, or Canadian citizens. Parliament is imagined to possess the ultimate lawmaking authority over all its citizens. A fundamental assumption underpinning the law governing Native people is that Parliament has the authority to pass laws governing Native people without their consent. The state, in other words, is a given. How did this assumption, the supremacy of Parliament, come to be embedded in Canadian legal thought, so much so that it rarely is questioned in constitutional discourse surrounding First Nations?

In the period of colonial expansion, it was accepted practice among European nations that the first to discover 'vacant' land acquired sovereignty over that land to the exclusion of other potential discoverers (Keller, Lissitzyn, and Mann 1938; Jennings 1963). In the case of populated land, sovereignty was acquired by the discovering nation not by simple settlement, but by conquest or cession (Brownlie 1990). One would assume that for England or France to claim sovereignty over parts of North America, they would have to enter into treaties with the indigenous population whereby the indigenous population would agree to submit to the sovereign authority of the settling nation, the alternative being the conquest of the indigenous population and forced compliance with the sovereign authority of the settling nation. It was also accepted practice, however, that populated land would be deemed vacant if its inhabitants did not meet certain standards. Initially the standard was a sectarian one: Is the indigenous population sufficiently Christian? If so, then sovereignty over that population could not be acquired by the simple discovery of the land. The standard then shifted to a secular inquiry into the degree of 'civilization' possessed by the indigenous population (Crawford 1978).

On both counts the indigenous population of North America failed, in the eyes of European nations (Williams 1990). Chief Justice John Marshall of the United States Supreme Court in *Johnson v. M'Intosh* (1823), for example, noted that the European justification for the assertion of territorial sovereignty in the face of an indigenous population rested on the view that the North American Indians were 'heathens': 'the character and religion of [North American's] inhabitants afforded an apology for considering them as a people over whom the superior genius of Europe might claim an ascendancy. The potentates of the old world found no difficulty in convincing themselves that they made ample compensation to the inhabitants of the new, by bestowing on them civilization and Christianity, in exchange for unlimited independence' (1823: 573). Thus, the law deemed North America vacant, and sovereignty was acquired by the mere fact of discovery. Native difference, in other words, in fact, Native inferiority, was the justification for the assertion of sovereignty by discovery by European nations. Native people were constructed as the other, and as inferior to the colonizing powers. Native inferiority provided the justification for treating Native people as subjects of the Crown. Sovereignty was asserted over the indigenous population by a denial of formal equality of peoples by the colonizing powers. Inequality of peoples was asserted by seizing upon Native difference and devaluing Native difference. Thus, the rhetoric of justification supporting the assertion of sovereignty was one which relied on Native difference. A basic organizing category of the Anglo-Canadian legal imagination, namely, that Canada enjoys sovereign legislative and executive authority over its indigenous inhabitants, ultimately rests on a denial that Native peoples are the same as or equal to non-Native peoples. Difference is asserted and devalued in order to legitimate the assertion of Canadian sovereignty.

Nowhere in the jurisprudence devoted to the distribution of legislative authority between Parliament and provincial legislatures is there any sustained examination of the legitimacy of the assertion of Canadian sovereignty over First Nations beyond the reasons alluded to by Chief Justice Marshall in *Johnson v. M'Intosh*. Working well within the boundaries of the Anglo-Canadian legal imagination, courts have never seriously questioned Canadian sovereignty over Native people. The law governing the distribution of legislative authority, subject to the recent constitutional recognition and affirmation of 'existing aboriginal and treaty rights' in section 35(1) of the Constitution Act, 1982, permits Parliament and provincial legislatures to pass laws regulating the life and culture of Native people without Native consent. Native consent is either assumed or deemed irrelevant in the law governing the distribution of authority over Native people. The issue underlying every dispute over jurisdiction in matters pertaining to Native people is not whether the state has authority to regulate incidents of Native title, but rather which level of government is entitled to regulate the matter in dispute. The underlying assumption is that Native title is subject to legislative regulation and extinguishment. Principles governing relations between levels of government accept without question a relationship of sovereign and subject between the Canadian state and Native peoples. The law governing the division of power over Native people is therefore premised on a hierarchical relationship between the state and Native people, with the former enjoying sovereign power over the latter.

Acceptance and denial of Native difference legitimate not only the assertion of legislative authority over Native people, but also the distribution of that authority between Parliament and provincial legislatures by the Canadian judiciary. The distribution of legislative authority is effected through a process of judicial interpretation that vacillates between a vision of Native people as different from non-Native people and one which sees Native people as similar to non-Native people. The boundary between federal and provincial jurisdiction over Native people is identified by reference to Native difference. The acceptance and denial of Native difference work to determine the scope of federal and provincial sovereignty over Native people and to maintain a hierarchical relationship between Native people and the Canadian state.

To illustrate, section 91(24) of the Constitution Act, 1867 confers on Parliament jurisdiction over 'Indians, and Lands reserved for the Indians.' In *Reference re Term 'Indians'* (1939), section 91(24) was interpreted to authorize Parliament to single out Native people, including Inuit peoples, and treat them differently than non-Native people. Section 91(24) also provides the constitutional authority for the Indian Act (1985) and other federal statutes that single out Native people for special treatment. The Indian Act provides for the establishment of band councils and the management and protection of

Indian lands and moneys, and defines certain Indian rights such as exemption from taxation in certain circumstances and entitlements to band membership and Indian status (Woodward 1989).

Parliament is also entitled to pass laws pursuant to other federal heads of power listed in the Constitution Act, 1867 and treat Native people the same as non-Native people. That federal legislation passed pursuant to a head of power other than section 91(24) applies to Native people is illustrated by *R. v. Derriksan* (1977), which involved a dispute between a Native person and fisheries officials. Derriksan was apprehended fishing in a certain area without a licence, contrary to provincial regulations passed pursuant to the federal Fisheries Act (1970). Derriksan argued that he was exercising his common law aboriginal right to fish in the area. The Supreme Court of Canada dismissed the argument on the basis that even if Derriksan was correct in asserting an aboriginal right to fish in the waters in question, Parliament has jurisdiction to regulate aboriginal rights not only by virtue of section 91(24) of the Constitution Act, 1867, but also by virture of other heads of power in section 91. The Court held the Fisheries Act, enacted pursuant to section 91(12) of the Constitution Act, 1867, which confers on Parliament jurisdiction over 'Sea Coast and Inland Fisheries,' to be applicable to Native people despite the fact that the law is not in relation to 'Indians, and Lands reserved for the Indians.' Parliament therefore is entitled to have its laws, passed under heads of power other than section 91(24), apply to Native people as well as non-Native people. Parliament, in other words, is entitled to ignore Native difference and treat Native people the same as non-Native people. It is also entitled, by virtue of section 91(24), to pass laws which single out Native people and treat Native people differently than non-Native people.

By contrast, a provincial legislature is not entitled to single out Native people and treat them differently than non-Native people. Legislation to this effect would be legislation in relation to 'Indians' and therefore *ultra vires* the province. This is illustrated by *R. v. Sutherland* (1980), in which the Court held that section 49 of Manitoba's Wildlife Act (1970) was *ultra vires* the province because it singled out and therefore was a law in relation to Native people. At issue in *Sutherland* was a memorandum of agreement between the federal and provincial governments designed to transfer from the federal government to the province all ungranted lands within the province. The memorandum of agreement stated that provincial fish and game laws would not apply to Native people seeking to hunt and fish on unoccupied Crown lands or on lands on which Native people had a right of access. Section 49 of Manitoba's Wildlife Act deemed a huge amount of Crown land to be occupied, thereby eliminating the authority that the memorandum of agreement gave to Native people to hunt and fish on the land in question. In the Court's view, provincial jurisdiction over property and civil rights does not entitle a province to single out Native people and treat them differently than non-Native people; since section 49 was aimed at Native people, it was *ultra vires* the province.

Despite the fact that a province cannot seek to regulate Native people by singling them out and treating them differently than non-Native people, a province, generally speaking, is entitled to treat Native people the same as non-Native people and regulate their affairs by laws of 'general application.' In *Kruger and Manuel v. The Queen* (1977), for example, at issue was whether a provincial game law applied to non-treaty Natives hunting off a reserve on unoccupied Crown land. Since the legislation had a uniform territorial operation and a valid provincial purpose, it was held to be a law of general application. Though a province is entitled to treat Native people the same as non-Native people and regulate Native affairs by laws of 'general application,' the Court noted that provincial authority in this regard is not unlimited. In the words of Dickson C.J., 'the line is crossed ... when an enactment, though in relation to another matter, by its effect, impairs the status or capacity' of Native people (1977: 110). A similar test was articulated by Justice Beetz in *Four B Manufacturing v. United Garment Workers of America* (1979), where he spoke of provincial laws of general application that touch on matters which are 'inherently Indian' or 'regulate Indians *qua* Indians' (1979: 398). In such cases, the law, despite its general applicability, will be held inapplicable to Native people.

Thus, a province is not entitled to single out Native people and treat them differently than non-Native people, nor is a province, under the guise of similar treatment, entitled to regulate Native peoples' essential difference. Difficulties arise, however, when the judiciary is asked to provide a precise location for this difference. Should it refer to attributes which are associated with the legal definition of 'Indian' or should difference be located elsewhere, for example, in Native culture or history? The former embraces a thin legal definition of aboriginal identity and leaves the provinces free to subject Native people to norms and values that are alien to Native culture so long as they are embodied in laws of general application and do not affect the legal status of Native people. In *Kruger and Manuel*, for example, the Court not only held that the provincial game law was a law of general application but also that it did not 'impair the status or capacity' of Native people. In *Four B Manufacturing*, a similar conclusion was reached with respect to provincial labour legislation. In both cases, few reasons were offered for the conclusion, though few are needed if by 'status and capacity' the Court means to refer to those attributes which make Native people Native in the eyes of the law. Provincial game laws, like provincial labour legislation, do not threaten 'Indian status ... [or] rights so closely connected with Indian status that they should be regarded as necessary incidents of status such for instance as registrability, membership in a band, the right to participate in the election of chiefs and band councils, reserve privileges, etc.' (1977).

If by status and capacity, however, one means to refer to the ability of Native people to engage in the cultural practices which help to constitute their individual and collective identities, provincial game laws do threaten the status and capacity of Native people for whom hunting and fishing is a central aspect of their Native identity. To reduce the meaning of status and capacity to its legal attributes leaves the provinces free to eliminate all that constitutes Native difference apart the formal shell of legal status, so long as this process of elimination occurs through laws of general application. To attempt to provide a rich definition of aboriginal difference, however, presents judges with the dilemma that they, and not First Nations themselves, are naming and thus constituting aboriginal identity. Aboriginal identity becomes imagined as something that can be discovered through legal inquiry, thereby displacing or at least disrupting individual and communal processes of negotiation over questions of aboriginal identity. In the words of Martha Minow, 'the use of a specific notion of identity to resolve a legal dispute can obscure the complexity of lived experiences while imposing the force of the state behind the selected notion of identity' (1991: 111).

As evidenced by this cursory review, principles designed to effect the distribution of authority between Parliament and provincial legislatures are founded on an unquestioned belief in the authority of the Canadian state to pass laws that affect First Nations without their consent. Judicial acceptance of federal authority over Native people is based on the view that the Constitution Act, 1867 authorizes Parliament and provincial legislatures to pass laws affecting Native people and that, by implication, Native people surrendered their sovereignty to the overarching authority of European monarchs upon the settlement of the continent. The legitimacy of this assumption is never seriously questioned by those entrusted with distributing the legislative power entailed by the assertion of territorial sovereignty. Ultimately grounded on notions of Native inferiority, the assertion of territorial sovereignty had the effect of subjecting indigenous forms of self-government to the legislative authority of the colonies.

Continued reliance on discovery to ground the legitimacy of traditional understandings of the Constitution Act, 1867 is deeply problematic (Slattery 1991). As illustrated by Chief Justice Marshall's reasons in *Johnson v. M'Intosh*, historical justifications for the assertion of territorial sovereignty are based on unacceptable notions of Native inferiority. The judiciary must begin to construct principles that accept the fact that Native people did not surrender their sovereignty or pre-existing forms of government by the mere fact of European settlement (Asch and Macklem 1991). The law governing the distribution of legislative authority over Native people ought to eliminate the interpretive obstacles currently in place that permit extensive federal and provincial regulation of Native people without native consent, and construct principles governing the distribution of authority to allow for the ability of Native people themselves to pass laws governing their individual and collective lives (Ryder 1991).

The assumption of Canadian sovereignty is central to legal ways of understanding, knowing, and assessing Native peoples' claims for greater control over their individual and collective identities. Aboriginal claims are assessed by a legal imagination that does not question the legitimacy of the assertion of Canadian sovereignty. First Nations sovereignty, in the strong sense, is unimaginable in the context of current legal ways of understanding. Claims of self-government that threaten traditional understandings of Canadian sovereignty are immediately rejected as implausible, beyond the pale, and unacceptable. Connor's insight into the reaction that ethnonationalist claims engender in state authorities is especially apt in the context of claims that challenge the legislative supremacy of the Canadian state. The state *is* imagined as a given; as such, the very subject that First Nations claims put into question – Canadian sovereignty – is seen as 'incontestable' (Connor 1973: 12).

PROPERTY RELATIONS

A central tenet of Anglo-Canadian property law is that the right of ownership carries with it a right to use and enjoyment of the land in question and a right to exclude others from entering onto one's land. Underpinning Anglo-Canadian conceptions of land ownership, however, is the prior assumption that property owners possess and own their land as a result of a grant from the Crown. The Crown is imagined in English property law as the original owner of all lands of the realm. This notion of underlying Crown title is fundamental to Anglo-Canadian property law. Kent McNeil has written that Crown title was originally developed as a fiction to legitimate feudal land holdings in England (1989). In order to rationalize and legitimate feudal landholdings, the law developed the fictions that the Crown was the original possessor and owner of all the lands of the realm, and that possessors and owners of land enjoyed rights of possession and ownership as a result of grants from the Crown. Since the law had imagined the Crown as granting lands to landholders, the Crown was no longer the full owner of granted land. Ownership, or fee simple, passed as a result of these grants to the landholder. This was not true in fact; the Crown was not the original possessor and therefore owner of the land, and by and large there were not actual grants effected by the Crown to landholders. These were fictions developed to rationalize and explain the pattern of landholdings in England. The concept of Crown title, however, was imported to the colonial context by the judiciary. As a result the Crown was imagined as the original possessor and therefore owner of all of the lands in North America over which England asserted territorial sovereignty (McNeil 1989).

Underlying Crown title was imported into the colonial context by a rhetoric of justification that saw Native people essentially the same as non-Native people. In *Johnson v. M'Intosh* (1823), Chief Justice Marshall not only addressed the legitimacy of asserting territorial sovereignty over an indigenous population, but also the question of underlying title to land. It was one thing to recognize that discovery entitles the discovering nation to assert sovereignty over Native people and an exclusive right to acquire Native land from Native people as against other European nations, and that this right of acquisition affects the freedom of Native people to alienate their lands to third parties. It was another to conclude that discovery actually vests underlying title to land in the discoverer as against the original inhabitants of the land. Adhering to the former entails only that the sovereign power is authorized to obtain ownership of the land over which sovereignty is asserted in accordance with its domestic laws govering title to land and ownership of real property.

Although his judgment occasionally appears to acknowledge the difference between territorial sovereignty and title to land, Marshall C.J. unfortunately blurred the distinction in his enlistment of the royal prerogative as support for his conclusion that the federal government had valid title to the land in question. He referred to 'the theory of the British constitution,' which, in his words, provides that 'all vacant lands are vested in the crown, as representing the nation; and the exclusive power to grant them is admitted to reside in the crown, as a branch of the royal prerogative' (1823: 595). English constitutional theory, according to Marshall C.J., made 'no distinction ... between vacant lands and lands occupied by Indians'; title to both was vested in the Crown (1823: 596). Since title to land vested in the Crown, it could not vest with the indigenous populations: 'an absolute title to lands cannot exist, at the same time, in different persons, or in different governments' (1823: 588). In Marshall's view, since title to vacant land and lands occupied by Native peoples vests with the Crown, the Crown is entitled to grant such lands to third parties. Marshall C.J. was then able to characterize the Indian interest in land as 'a right of occupancy,' subject to the 'absolute' power of the Crown to extinguish that right (1823: 588). Marshall C.J. was unwilling to acknowledge any difference between Native people and non-Native people which might justify special treatment with respect to the Crown prerogative. Invoking the royal prerogative to support the conclusion that the Crown possesses title to Native land treats Native people as if they were British subjects, and ignores the fact that Native people were original inhabitants of the land in question and that such land was not in fact vacant. Marshall C.J., in other words, denied Native difference to support the assertion of underlying Crown title to Native lands.

Marshall C.J. subsequently changed his views about the effect of the assertion of territorial sovereignty on land ownership patterns, ultimately opting for the more cautious position that discovery vests only an exclusive right of acquisition of indigenous lands as against other potential discoverers, as in *Worcester v. Georgia* (1832). Canadian courts, however, have not moved away from the notion of underlying Crown title to ancestral lands. Instead of viewing Native people as enjoying underlying title to ancestral lands with discovery vesting a mere right in the Crown to acquire Native title, Canadian courts assume that underlying title vests in the Crown and that as a result aboriginal title can be extinguished by the Crown absent Native consent and absent any compensatory obligation. Subject to the impact of section 35(1) of the Constitution Act, 1982, the common law assumption that the Crown enjoys underlying title to unsurrendered Native land permits the Crown to extinguish Native proprietary interests without consent and without compensation and renders Native peoples' relations to their ancestral lands contingent on the goodwill of the Crown.

In an early case indirectly involving Native title, *St Catherines Milling and Lumber Co. v. The Queen* (1888), the Privy Council delineated the nature of the Native interest at common law in lands not surrendered by treaty to the Crown. The issue arose in the context of a dispute between Ontario and the federal government over the legality of a logging permit issued by the federal government to St Catherines Milling. The federal government argued that it possessed the authority to issue a permit because it had obtained title to the land in question by virtue of a treaty it entered into with the Ojibway nation in 1873, in which the Ojibway people agreed to 'cede, release, surrender, yield up, transfer and relinquish' specified lands to the Crown forever in return for, among other benefits, the recognition of limited hunting and fishing rights and reserve lands. The federal government also relied on section 91(24) of the Constitution Act, 1867, which gives exclusive jurisdiction to Parliament over 'Lands reserved for the Indians.' The province argued that it possessed underlying title to the land in question by virtue of section 109 of the Constitution Act, which provides that all lands belonging to the province at the time of Confederation continue to belong to the province. In dismissing the federal government's arguments, Lord Watson distinguished between the federal right to legislate with respect to Native land and provincial proprietary rights. Under section 91(24), the federal government is entitled to enter into treaties with respect to Native land and to extinguish Native title. Should Native people be divested of their proprietary interest in land, however, title to the land remains with the provincial Crown by virtue of section 109 of the Constitution Act.

In so holding, Lord Watson made reference to the nature and extent of the Native interest in terms similar to those articulated by Marshall C.J. in *Johnson v. M'Intosh*. Lord Watson spoke of a 'personal and usufructory right' attaching to Native people with respect to unsurrendered land, 'dependent on the good will of the Sovereign' (1888: 54). This 'unsufructory right' is a right of use and possession subject to surrender to or extinguishment by the Crown; in his words, 'there has been all along vested in the Crown a substantial and paramount estate, underlying the Indian title, which became a plenum dominium whenever that title was surrendered or otherwise extinguished' (1888: 77). *St Catherines Milling* thus assumes the dependent proprietary relationship which Chief Justice Marshall sought to justify in *Johnson v. M'Intosh*: namely, that notwithstanding the fact that Native people were the original occupants of the lands, the Crown has underlying title and is entitled to extinguish the Native interest without Native consent. The result is that property law imagines the Crown to hold underlying title to Indian land and the Native relation to land to be 'dependent upon the good will of the Sovereign.'

Canadian property law thus imagines the Crown to be the original possessor and therefore the owner of all of Canada, just as in England, with one critical difference: it does not also imagine the aboriginal population as owning ancestral lands as a result of grants from the Crown. While in England the fiction of underlying Crown title was accompanied by the fiction of a system of grants to private owners, thereby having the effect of legitimating and rationalizing then-existing landholdings, only one-half of this equation was imported to Canada. The Crown was imagined as originally owning all of Canada, and the prior occupants were not imagined as subsequently owning their land as a result of a series of fictional Crown grants. The importation of the fiction of Crown title into the Canadian context, instead of working to legitimate then-current landholdings as it did in England, worked to severely disrupt then-current aboriginal landholdings in Canada. The Crown and not the aboriginal population was imagined as owning the land. Since the law did not imagine the Crown to have granted the land away to the aboriginal population, it was free to grant the land to whomever it pleased, which it did: to settlers, mining companies, forestry companies, and the like.

That this is the case was borne out by the famous split decision of the Supreme Court of Canada in *Calder v. A.G.B.C.* (1973). *Calder* involved an action brought by members of the Nishga Nation on the coast of British Columbia requesting a declaration that their title to certain lands in the province had never been lawfully extinguished. Despite the fact that the Nishga people had not surrendered the lands in question by treaty, the provincial Crown had made numerous grants with respect to the lands for development purpose: mining, petroleum exploration, tree farming, and forestry, and fee simple grants. The Nishga people claimed that they possessed aboriginal title to the land by virtue of the fact that they had been occupants 'from time immemorial.'

The Court dismissed the Nishga claim, with a narrow procedural holding by Pigeon J. deciding the appeal. The other members of the Court were split on the question of extinguishment of title. Judson J., with whom Martland and Ritchie JJ. concurred, argued that whatever interest the Nishga may have had at common law, it had been extinguished by legislation and proclamation prior to British Columbia's joining Confederation. Referring to United States cases which rely on Marshall C.J. for the proposition that ' "the exclusive right of the United States to extinguish" Indian title has never been doubted,' Judson J. was quick to conclude that in the present case 'the sovereign authority elected to exercise complete dominion over the lands in question, adverse to any right of occupancy which the Nishga Tribe might have had, when, by legislation, it opened up such lands for settlement, subject to the reserves of land set aside for Indian occupation' (1973: 160–1, 167). Compensation, in Judson J.'s view, is owed only when there is a 'statutory direction to pay' – in other words, when the legislature so decides (1973: 167).

Justice Hall wrote a powerful dissent, concurred in by Spence and Laskin JJ., in which he argued that Nishga title was not extinguished by colonial proclamations and legislative enactments. Reacting against the tenor of historical documentation which imagined Native people to be 'in effect a subhuman species' (1973: 169), Justice Hall sought to expand the nature of the Indian proprietary interest within the confines established by *St Catherines Milling* and Marshall C.J.'s vision in *Johnson v. M'Intosh*. Hall J. rooted the Native interest in the common law of property and invoked the common law principle that 'possession is of itself at common law proof of ownership' (1973: 185). The evidence clearly established that the Nishga people were prima facie 'owners of the lands that have been in their possession from time immemorial' (1973: 190). Hall J. nevertheless appeared to accept that the Crown possesses underlying title to Indian land to the extent that he refers to, and seemingly accepts, the fact that the Nishga did 'not deny the right of the Crown to dispossess them' (1973: 174). In his view, the Native interest in land could lawfully be extinguished by legislation without consent and presumably without compensation, yet he would require a legislative intention to extinguish Indian title to be 'clear and plain.' Without a clear expression of intent, Native title would continue to exist. His acceptance of an underlying Crown title to Native lands appears to contemplate the further possibility of executive extinguishment was well.

Despite their differences, both judgments remain true to the relationship of dependence enshrined in the legal principles articulated by Marshall C.J. in *Johnson v. M'Intosh*. Judson J. is explicit that any property rights Native people may enjoy are contingent on the discretion of the Crown, and that the Crown is entitled to extinguish Native interests at any time without consent and without compensation. Hall J. adopts a similar framework of understanding to the extent that he envisages that the Crown or a legislature is entitled to extinguish aboriginal title without consent and compensation as long as it expresses a clear intent to do so. While Hall J. is sympathetic to aboriginal forms of life, neither Hall J. nor Judson J. questions that executive or legislative action can extinguish what permits these forms of life to flourish: Native use and enjoyment of land.

Canadian law governing First Nations interests in ancestral lands therefore consists of a set of legal principles that establishes and maintains a legal relationship of dependence between Native people and the Canadian state. First Nations are restricted to use and enjoyment of unsurrendered ancestral or reserve land, and, subject to section 35(1) of the Constitution Act, 1982, the Crown holds underlying title to such land and thereby enjoys the right to unilaterally extinguish aboriginal title. This relationship of dependence has been supported and sustained by a vision of Native people as similar to non-Native people. Viewing Native people as similar to non-Native people in the context of property law enables the judiciary to avoid exploring the legal implications of the fact that aboriginal people are the original inhabitants of the continent. The law erases this aspect of aboriginal identity from its understanding of aboriginal legal interests in land. In so doing, property law ensures that geographic borders and property rules do not threaten basic organizing categories of the Anglo-Canadian legal imagination. The result is that First Nations are severely restricted from developing and expressing their unique identities in the context of their relations with ancestral lands.

CONCLUSION

The assertion of territorial sovereignty was supported or legitimated by an emphasis on Native difference, whereas the assertion of Crown title was supported or legitimated by an emphasis on Native similarity. The combination of these two developments is a legal imagination strongly resistant to the aspiration of Native peoples to have greater control over their individual and collective identities. Built into the very premises of the legal imagination brought to bear in the assessment of claims to greater autonomy for First Nations are premises that are diametrically opposed to the aspiration. Property law severely restricts Native peoples' abilities to institutionalize and render into legal form their unique relations with land. The continued assertion of Canadian sovereignty severely restricts First Nations ability to pass laws governing their lives free from external interference. Walker Connor's claim that the state is a given by those in power when faced with ethnonationalist claims rings especially true in the context of the law governing Native peoples in Canada.

In order for there to be any real development toward the institutionalization of Native peoples' aspirations for greater control over their individual and collective identities, contexts must open up where, in Walker Connor's words, 'the political integrity of the sovereign territory' can be rendered contestable (1973: 120). Challenges are currently occurring in a number of different contexts: in legislatures, the media, parliamentary inquiries, the courts, international tribunals, as well as at the blockades. Property law must acknowledge Native difference beyond the limited notion of a usufructory right and permit the freeing up of the multiple processes by which aboriginal identities are constructed out of individual and communal encounters with nature and land. To do so requires a significant shift away from the fiction that the Crown owns underlying title to all of Canada and the notion that aboriginal interests in land rest on the continued goodwill of the Canadian state.

As of 1982, an interpretive site for debate over the assumptions underpinning constitutional regulation of First Nations has been created. Section 35(1) of the Constitution Act, 1982 recognizes and affirms 'existing aboriginal and treaty rights of the aboriginal peoples of Canada.' Laws that interfere with existing aboriginal rights are now subject to judicial scrutiny (*R. v. Sparrow* (1990)). Section 35(1) creates the opportunity for requiring that constitutional discourse include an assessment of the legitimacy of the assertion of Canadian sovereignty. In order to determine whether Native forms of self-government, forms of government that existed prior to settlement, continue to exist as section 35(1) rights, a determination of the legitimacy or lawfulness of the assertion of Canadian sovereignty over the indigenous population is required (Asch and Macklem 1991). The scope of section 35(1) is dependent on an assessment of the legitimacy of the assertion of Canadian sovereignty. Whether or not, or to what extent, Canada exercises sovereign authority over its indigenous population, is now a question of domestic constitutional law, and reasons must be offered for the assertion. It is no longer acceptable to rely on the reasons relied on by the settling nations. Native difference and inferiority are no longer constitutionally acceptable justifications for the continued assertion of Canadian sovereignty. It may well be that there are valid reasons for the partial assertion of Canadian sovereignty over Canada's First Nations, that some matters ought to fall within federal control, but it also may well be that First Nations ought to be vested with authority over those matters or aspects of social and political life that constitute their difference. This will require a redrawing of the constitutional imagination, an imagination that currently sees political sovereignty, according to Walker Connor, as incontestable, toward one which recognizes the need to construct spaces in which First Nations can participate in the formation of laws that govern their lives and define their own identities.

Acknowledgments

I would like to thank Aly Feltes and Ted Chamberlin for their invaluable assistance and Kent McNeil for his helpful comments on an earlier draft. Many of the ideas presented in this paper are explored at greater length in an essay entitled 'First Nations Self-Government and the Borders of the Canadian Legal Imagination' (1991), *McGill Law Journal* 36(2): 382.

REFERENCES

Asch, Michael, and Patrick Macklem. 1991. 'Aboriginal Rights and Canadian Sovereignty: An Essay on *R. v. Sparrow.' Alberta Law Review* 29(2): 498

Brownlie, I. 1990. *Principles of Public International Law*, 4th ed. Oxford: Clarendon Press

Calder v. A.G.B.C. 1973. S.C.R. 313, (1973), 34 D.L.R. (3d) 145

Clifford, James. 1988. *The Predicament of Culture: Twentieth-Century Ethnography, Literature, and Art.* Cambridge: Harvard University Press

Connor, Walker. 1973. 'The Politics of Ethnonationalism.' *Journal of International Affairs* 27(1): 1

Crawford, James. 1979. *The Creation of States in International Law.* Oxford: Clarendon Press

Four B Manufacturing v. United Garment Workers of America. 1979. 102 D.L.R. (3d) 385 (S.C.C.)

Jennings, R.Y. 1963. *The Acquisition of Territory in International Law.* Manchester: Manchester University Press

Johnson v. M'Intosh. 1823. 21 U.S. (8 Wheat.) 543

Keller, A.S., O.J. Lissitzyn, and F.J. Mann. 1938. *Creation of Rights of Sovereignty through Symbolic Acts, 1400–1800*. New York: Columbia University Press

Kruger and Manuel v. The Queen. 1978. 1 S.C.R. 104, (1977), 75 D.L.R. (3d) 434

Macklem, Patrick. 1991. 'First Nations Self-Government and the Borders of the Canadian Legal Imagination.' *McGill Law Journal* 36(2): 382

McNeil, Kent. 1989. *Common Law Aboriginal Title*. Oxford: Clarendon Press

McMillan, A.D. 1988. *Native Peoples and Cultures of Canada: An Anthropological Overview*. Toronto: Douglas and McIntyre

Minow, Martha. 1987. 'The Supreme Court 1986 Term – Foreword: Justice Engendered.' *Harvard Law Review* 101: 10

– 1991. 'Identities.' *Yale Journal of Law and Humanities* 3(1): 97

R. v. Derriksan. 1976. 71 D.L.R. (3d) 159 (S.C.C.)

R. v. Sparrow. 1990. 1 S.C.R. 1075, 70 D.L.R. (4th) 385

R. v. Sutherland. 1980. 2 S.C.R. 451, (1981), 113 D.L.R. (3d) 374

Reference re Term 'Indians.' 1939. S.C.R. 104

Ryder, Bruce. 1991. 'The Demise and Rise of the Classical Paradigm in Canadian Federalism: Promoting Autonomy for the Provinces and First Nations.' *McGill Law Journal* 36(2): 308

St Catherines Milling and Lumber Co. v. The Queen. 1888. 14 A.C. 46 (P.C.)

Slattery, Brian. 1991. 'Aboriginal Sovereignty and Imperial Claims.' *Osgoode Hall Law Journal* 29(4): 681

Williams Jr., Robert A. 1990. *The American Indian in Western Legal Thought: The Discourses of Conquest*. New York: Oxford University Press

Woodward, Jack. 1989. *Native Law*. Toronto: Carswell

Worcester v. Georgia. 1832. 31 U.S. (6 Pet.) 515

CHAPTER 2

Aboriginal Self-Government and Canadian Constitutional Identity: Building Reconciliation

Michael Asch

Canadians are at a pivotal moment in our constitutional history. Notwithstanding views by Premier Rae (1990) and others that the economy or some other issue is the number one priority in the minds of voters, now is the time when we must begin to act on resolving the crisis of community that besets us.

The crisis of community is itself a crisis in our constitutional approach to resolving one major dilemma of the modern nation-state: the relationship between the collective political rights of minority collectivities with political rights based on the principle of majority rule. At the same moment we are confronted by the need to consider the accommodation of two distinct kinds of minority collectivity within Canada: the regional and the ethnonational (Connor 1973). Minorities with voices that appeal for an immediate reappraisal of our institutions include those from Quebec, the West, the North, and aboriginal peoples. For each, at least in principle, one alternative to the status quo is separation and, thus, independence from the majority. For both regional and ethnonational minorities in Canada, there are alternatives to the choice between the constitutional status quo and separation. My research has focused primarily on those related to ethnonational minorities. This research has led me to explore the concept of 'consociation' as it has been described in anthropological theory (Smith 1969).

The term 'consociation' was developed almost simultaneously in anthropology and political science (Lijphart 1977) to mean two slightly different things (Asch 1984). In the anthropological view, consociation represents one of the fundamental ways in which state ideology identifies citizens with respect to ethnonational identity. In states that follow 'universalistic' ideology (such as the United States of America) state ideology identifies citizens solely as individuals and recognizes no ethnonational minority communities. In contrast, states that follow 'consociational' ideology identify citizens both as individuals and as members of various ethnonational communities and act to ensure equality of protection for both individual and minority ethnonational collective rights (for example, see Van Dyke 1980 regarding Belgium). In the modern world, liberal-democratic states are commonly based on universalistic premises and only rarely on consociational ones.

In order to better understand the nature of consociational states and how they act to protect collective political rights, I have found it useful to divide them into two distinct types (Asch 1990). While each results in the protection of the collective political rights of specified ethnonational minorities, each does it by use of different constitutional principles. As a result, state ideology with respect to the rights of ethnonational minorities acquires very different characteristics.

The first type I define as *direct* consociation. Here state ideology expressly acknowledges the existence of various ethnonational collectivities (as, for example, in its constitutional charter), and thus protection is afforded explicitly to specified and named ethnonational communities.

The second type I define as *indirect* consociation. In this case, state ideology does not explicitly recognize or protect minority ethnonational communities. Rather, its ideology espouses the philosophy of universalism. Protection of specific ethnonational minorities is created as a consequence of other principles. One method of achieving this goal is to divide powers between federal and provincial levels of government and then to ensure that the specified minority ethnonational collectivity forms a majority within a particular provincial jurisdiction. In contrast to a direct consociation, in this form the constitutional charter would not refer explicitly to any ethnonational collectivity. Thus, the ethnonational minority's control could be maintained only so long as the constitutional division of powers remained unchanged and, in real political terms, only so long as it retained a majority status within a recognized political jurisdiction.

In my view, Canada, as the division of powers has been organized through the Constitution Act, 1867, represents an attempt to construct an indirect consociation with respect to the French fact as it exists in Quebec. Thus, Canada espouses an ideology of universalism in that there are no named and recognized ethnonational collectivities in the constitution. However, because the majority of the population of Quebec belongs to a distinct ethnonational community, the division of powers between provincial and federal levels as well as the sanctity of the borders of Quebec provides a de facto consociational result.

This result represents a judicious compromise. From the francophone point of view, Canada can be ideologically constructed to be a direct consociation between the French and the 'English.' From an anglophone point of view, Canada can be ideologically constructed to be a universalistic state that happens to be organized under principles of federalism.

While this compromise may have produced stability for over a century, it is now generating instability. This was exemplified in the Meech Lake debate. If Canadian constitutional identity had been already based on principles of direct consociation, then neither the naming of Quebec as a distinct society within Canada nor the need to protect minority collective rights (such as through the law controlling language of signs) would have been so controversial in anglophone Canada. However, as state ideology, at least as constructed by anglophone Canada, adheres to the philosophy of universalism, the naming of Quebec as a distinct society as well as the recognition of a need to protect collective minority rights over individual rights was eschewed. I would argue that this situation was created in large measure because of the ambiguities in constitutional ideology inherent in the use of the principle of indirect consociation.

It is my view that the use of principles of direct consociation represents a better solution to the problem of minority–majority ethnonational relations than does the principle of universalism. Elsewhere, I discuss (Asch 1990) methods whereby the direct consociational approach (Asch 1984) may be used as a means to reconcile aboriginal collective political rights with a public government majority-rule system in the western Northwest Territories. Here I intend to focus on a related matter: the need to reconstitute our constitutional identity with regard to the political status of aboriginal nations that find themselves within Canada. In particular, I will address the assertion that aboriginal nations have an 'inherent' right to self-determination and self-government, and that this inherent right must find both practical and constitutional recognition by the Canadian state.

The nub of my concern is this. In my view, current constitutional ideology greatly devalues this proposition. It does so largely because, on an intellectual level, we have not accepted the principles of direct consociation and have not found a need, a will, or a means to work at resolving the matter of aboriginal self-government through principles of indirect consociation. Indeed, in our constitutional ideology, aboriginal peoples, as opposed to the French fact, represent one component among many ethnocultural communities, none of which, given the universalistic ideology that dominates thinking in 'non-French' Canada, should have any special collective political rights. But I go further. I argue that our espoused universalistic ideology in fact masks assumptions about the moral legitimacy of our occupation of Canada that have colonial and racist overtones. In other words, state ideology with respect to the aboriginal question not only runs counter to the reasonable resolution of legitimate political rights for aboriginal nations, but can be seen to give support to principles that are morally repugnant. Thus, I would argue that, if Canada (or Quebec, should it decide to separate) is ever to build a nation that can accommodate the aspirations of aboriginal nations, the ideology of universalism must be overturned.

The body of this paper is divided into two major sections. In the first, I discuss the constitutional ideology that orients Canadian constitutional thinking on aboriginal self-government in some detail. I focus here primarily on a textual examination of the Canadian Constitution Acts of 1867 and 1982, government policy in areas such as comprehensive land claims, and recent Supreme Court of Canada decisions such as in the *R. v. Sparrow* case (1990). In this context, I also address the view of the aboriginal nations with respect to their right to self-government and its recognition in the constitution. The second section deals more specifically with the ideological basis for the assertions of government. I close with a brief discussion of the implications of rejecting or accepting either party's position on the question of aboriginal political rights. Specifically, I will indicate that the approach to aboriginal self-government should be based on principles of direct consociation and how, given the form in which aboriginal nations suggest it will be expressed, this will help us to generate the very kind of process needed in order to promote reconciliation between peoples and regions in this country.

CANADIAN STATE IDEOLOGY AND ABORIGINAL POLITICAL RIGHTS

I have suggested above that Canadian state ideology masks assumptions about our occupation of Canada that have racist and colonial overtones. This is a serious charge, so let me hasten to add that I do not mean that Canadians are inherently racist or colonialist in their attitudes, nor that they would support a state ideology that would overtly espouse such principles. Rather, I believe that these attitudes flow mainly from our neglect of examining older historical assumptions about aboriginal nations and from some of the premises of universalism itself. In fact, I believe that Canadians in general, regardless where we reside or to which ethnonational collectivity we belong would find it morally repugnant to support a state that expressed such principles. This is one reason why I think the mere articulation of the racist and colonial implications of certain facets of current constitutional ideology will have a salutary effect on making necessary changes.

Let me begin by illustrating what I mean. I thought Canada had come a long way since British Columbia Chief Justice Davey felt comfortable in stating with regard to the aboriginal rights of the Nishga in 1970 (Asch 1984: 49): '[The Nishga] ... were at the time of settlement a very primitive people with few of the institutions of civilized society ... [Therefore], I have no evidence to justify a conclusion that the aboriginal rights claimed by the successors of these primitive peoples are of a kind that it should be assumed the Crown recognized them when it acquired the mainland of British Columbia by occupation.' In fact, I would mark the admonition by Supreme Court Justice Hall to Justice Davey's remarks as crucial to the development of our constitutional thinking about the place of aboriginal nations within Canada. He said (Asch 1984: 50): 'The assessment and interpretation of historical documents and enactments tendered in evidence must be approached in light of present-day research and knowledge, disregarding ancient concepts formulated when understanding of the customs and cultures of our original people was rudimentary and incomplete and when they were thought to be wholly without cohesion, laws, or culture, in effect a subhuman species ...' It is this approach, I believe, that is necessary to our rethinking of the pejorative assumptions and implications of our current state ideology with respect to accepting the premise of an inherent right to self-determination and self-government.

Yet, the problem remains, and not just intellectually. It has a practical effect on the world. The following is excerpted from the 'Statement of the Attorney-General of Canada's Position on Extinguishment, Diminution or Abandonment of Aboriginal Rights in the Claim Area' (Attorney-General of Canada 1989). It was filed in December of 1989 by the government in defence of a claim by the Gitksan–Wet'suwet'en Nation (referred to below as Gitksan). It says that regarding:

1 The plaintiffs' claim to ownership and jurisdiction over all the lands in the claim area.

The Attorney-General of Canada responds:

Ownership and jurisdiction constitute a claim to sovereignty. If the Plaintiffs ever had sovereignty, it was extinguished completely by the assertion of sovereignty by Great Britain.

What the second sentence actually suggests is that: (1) Canada doubts that the Gitksan were ever civilized enough to have sovereignty; but that (2) if they did have it, the mere assertion of sovereignty by Great Britain was enough to extinguish it. Such a line of argument is, in my view, racist and colonialist in spirit and intent. It flies not only in the face of the culturally relativist assumptions underlying Justice Hall's remarks cited above, but also, and perhaps more importantly, the spirit of relevant United Nations declarations on the rights of colonized peoples – declarations Canada itself is a party to. My point is that any constitutional ideology that enables the attorney-general of Canada to make such bald remarks is unacceptable and must be changed. I am arguing that the making of such assumptions in 1989 would not have been possible were it not for some inherent bias in the current way in which we conceptualize the incorporation of aboriginal nations into the Canadian state and society.

My question, then, is what is there in *current* constitutional thinking about the place of aboriginal nations within Canada that gives support to such a statement? My provisional answer, which is based on my reading of primary texts, such as the Constitution Acts of 1867 and 1982, and is admittedly impressionistic, follows below. But first, one point. There is, of course, a strong and growing literature that lays out the history of Canadian political thought and state policy on the topic. This history is important for an overall discussion of the evolution of constitutional thought on the topic. However, this is beyond the scope of this contribution. Here, I will focus on current thinking. I will do this primarily by examining a few basic sources, including some that are historical. I begin with the Constitution Act, 1867, which until 1982 was called the British North America Act, and is still commonly known by that name.

THE CONSTITUTION ACT, 1867

The Constitution Act, 1867, is our most fundamental constitutional document with respect to both the assertion of political 'dominion' over the land mass now called Canada and the distribution of sovereign power in its domain. This document, as is common knowledge (see, for example, Van Loon and Whittington 1987), indicates that the Canadian state is to be federal in nature with two levels of government, the federal and the provincial. It specifies clearly, primarily in sections 91, 92, and 93, the division of sovereign power between the two levels of government.

Section 91 describes, specifically, the areas of legislative authority held by the federal government. These include, among other things, the right to pass laws about the regulation of trade and commerce (part 2), about taxation (part 3), about currency (part 14), and about the criminal code (part 27).

Sections 92 and 93 describe the power to pass laws held by the provinces. These, among other matters, include in section 92: 'the Management and Sale of the Public Lands belonging to the Province and of the Timber and Wood thereon' (part 5), the establishment and maintenance of hospitals (part 7), property rights in the province (part 13), and 'Generally all Matters of a merely local or private Nature in the Province' (part 16). Section 93 deals with education and makes it primarily a provincial responsibility.

The preamble to the Constitution Act, 1867 makes it clear that the constitution was undertaken as an act of federal union by specific provinces in British North America. Thus, it assumes that the previous provincial authorities were 'sovereign' (under the Queen). It suggests that one primary goal of the act is to construct a 'Constitution similar in Principle to that of the United Kingdom' (Van Loon and Whittington 1987: 637). It is ahistorical in that it makes no mention of earlier conditions out of which the union is to emerge and is not 'ontological' for, unlike the Constitution Act, 1982, which begins with the words 'Whereas Canada is founded upon principles that recognize the supremacy of God and the rule of law,' it asserts no founding philosophical principles.

Aboriginal people are mentioned in only one place in the original British North America Act, in section 91(24). Section 91, which enumerates the powers of the federal government, specifically says (Van Loon and Whittington 1987: 864): 'the exclusive Legislative Authority of the Parliament of Canada extends to all Matters coming within the Classes of Subjects next hereinafter enumerated ...' One of these matters, found in subsection 24 is 'Indians and Lands reserved for the Indians (ibid. 666).' In other words, the BNA Act specifies that Indians and lands reserved for them fall under the exclusive legislative authority of the federal parliament. This subsection could be interpreted as meaning that it is only the federal government and not the provinces that has the authority to negotiate with Indians and to regulate Indian affairs after negotiations have resulted in treaties of mutual consent. Indeed, such an interpretation seems very plausible when one examines the Constitution Act, 1867 in light of the undertakings such as are found in the Royal Proclamation of 1763 and in the provision to deal with Native land claims contained in the Rupert's Land Act of 1870. Indeed, I would hope and expect that such and interpretation will ultimately prove definitive in our constitutional thought.

The fact is that this interpretation is not now definitive. An alternative interpretation would be that section 91(24) in fact asserts unilateral dominion over Indians and lands reserved for Indians, subject only to dealing fairly with their claims. Such a reading would rely, among other things, on the fact that the preamble to the 1867 document draws no attention to history but assumes the inherent sovereignty of the parties entering into confederation and from the very specific way in which that act divides all sovereignty within the dominion into either the federal or the provincial sphere. In other words, it relies on a decontextualized reading of the act and assumes that, whereas silence must be interpreted narrowly, the written word must be interpreted broadly. I believe that it is the use of such an interpretive frame that lies behind the remarks of the attorney-general of Canada cited above.

THE CONSTITUTION ACT, 1982

The Constitution Act, 1982 deals with a number of fundamental constitutional matters that include, most importantly, the rights of individual citizens, minority language education rights, and a method to amend the constitution itself. It begins, as I have suggested above, with a philosophical statement as a preamble which, to repeat, says (Van Loon and Whittington 1987: 697): 'Whereas Canada is founded upon principles that recognize the supremacy of God and the rule of law.' However, again, like the Constitution Act, 1867, it provides no historical context or justification for the assumption that Canada exists.

Three sections of the Constitution Act, 1982 make explicit reference to aboriginal peoples. The first is section 25. It states that (Van Loon and Whittington 1987: 703): 'The guarantee in this Charter of certain rights and freedoms shall not be construed so as to abrogate or derogate from any aboriginal, treaty or other rights or freedoms that pertain to the aboriginal peoples of Canada.' In other words, it protects the rights of aboriginal peoples from any legal interpretation that would diminish their force when they are in possible conflict with the application of the Charter of Rights and Freedoms.

The second is section 35. It defines the 'aboriginal peoples of Canada' as including Indians, Inuit, and Metis, a clause that is of particular importance to the Metis who previously were in a potentially ambiguous legal position regarding their status as aboriginal peoples. It also assures among other matters that the rights obtained through the settlement of modern land claims would be considered constitutionally equivalent to treaty rights and hence would find constitutional protection under the Constitution Act, 1982.

Finally, and most crucially, section 35 states that: 'The existing aboriginal and treaty rights of the aboriginal peoples of Canada are hereby recognized and affirmed' (Van Loon and Whittington 1987: 705). In other words, it unambiguously extends constitutional recognition to those aboriginal and treaty rights that are said to 'exist.' The Constitution Act, 1982, however, did not specify these rights. This was to be done, at least in part, through a series of conferences to be held under section 37. According to the act, each of these conferences was to include 'in its agenda constitutional matters that directly affect the aboriginal peoples of Canada' (Van Loon and Whittington 1987: 707).

The original version of the Constitution Act went on to state explicitly that the agenda was to include 'the identification and definition of the rights of those peoples to be included in the Constitution of Canada' (ibid.). However, this clause was dropped from versions subsequent to 17 April 1983. Nonetheless, it is clear from the constitutional discussions that took place under this section that the primary purpose of these conferences was still to identify and define aboriginal and treaty rights. This series of conferences ended in 1987. They failed to obtain agreement among the governments and the aboriginal leadership on the definition and identification of these rights. Therefore, the Constitution Act, 1982 remains silent on their specific content.

The question then becomes one of interpretation. It asks: What is the content of constitutionally entrenched aboriginal and treaty rights in the absence of positive language on the subject? A lot of intellectual effort has been expended on answering this question. However, for the sake of clarity, primary positions can be reduced to two.

The first represents the consensus of governments. It has been identified as the 'contingent right' position. This position, as I understand it, assumes the paramountcy of the Canadian state as the foundation of rights. Thus, it asserts that no aboriginal or treaty right can exist in a constitutionally entrenched sense unless and until it has been specifically recognized by Canada either through explicit acts of legislation or court interpretation. In other words, as Canada is paramount, aboriginal and treaty rights depend for their existence on formal recognition by the state. Hence, their constitutional existence is contingent upon such explicit recognition.

This interpretive framework places heavy reliance on the actual language of legislation and the courts. Thus, it would hold that the actual wording of the treaties with aboriginal nations was authoritative with respect to the constitutional interpretation of the contents of treaty rights. Equally, it would hold that actual legislation and/or court interpretation would be crucial to defining the content of existing aboriginal rights. And, it would assert that there is really very little content to these rights because, on the one hand, there was, with the possible exception of the Royal Proclamation of 1763 and the constitutional provisions for negotiating land claims, no specific legislation that put such rights into existence, and, on the other, court interpretations explicitly held at most that existing aboriginal rights include primarily the right to hunt and fish on unoccupied Crown land, subject to regulation by the Crown. This thesis is consistent with the presumption contained in the preambles of the two constitution acts as outlined above that Canada represents an initial condition of sovereignty over its land mass. Therefore, any aboriginal or treaty right must be contingent upon Canada's existence as a state and hence on Canada's express recognition of it. As 'sovereignty has yet to be expressly acknowledged by the state,' it cannot exist in a constitutional sense. Hence, this interpretive framework supports the views on the doubtful nature of aboriginal sovereignty and the legitimacy of a unilateral extinguishment through the assertion of sovereignty by Great Britain that were enunciated by the attorney-general of Canada in the case cited above.

The second position is the one espoused by aboriginal leaders. It has been termed the 'inherent right' position. It suggests that aboriginal rights came into existence before the Canadian state and can continue to exist independently of the creation of Canada. Thus, as these rights are inherent, they do not need to be given explicit legislative sanction to be put into effect. This implies that the main function of the words concerning 'existing' in section 35 was to incorporate recognition of these rights into the Canadian constitution. I will discuss this interpretation at more length below.

RECENT SUPREME COURT DECISIONS AND CONSTITUTIONAL INTERPRETATION

In the years since the passage of the Constitution Act, 1982, the Supreme Court has made a number of key decisions regarding the interpretation of aboriginal and treaty rights in light of provisions contained in section 35. Of these, three essential decisions were made in the spring of 1990. These are: *R. v. Horseman*, *R. v. Siuoi*, and *R. v. Sparrow*. In this brief overview, I will not examine even these three decisions in detail, but rather will focus primarily on the one that I interpret as most basic to the understanding of the nature of aboriginal and treaty rights with respect to the questions addressed in this paper. This is the *Sparrow* case.

In brief, the *Sparrow* case concerns an aboriginal right to fish in British Columbia for the Musqueam people, an aboriginal nation that never signed a treaty. The questions in this case of particular note to this discussion, then, are: whether this right existed before Canada did and, if so, whether it was automatically cancelled, either through Canada's assertion of sovereignty or through a valid legislative act of Canada or British Columbia, subsequent to Canada's assertion of sovereignty.

As the discussion that follows will show, the *Sparrow* case does provide strong support for the contention that aboriginal rights did exist before Canada and that they continue to exist despite the mere assertion of sovereignty by Canada or acts of Parliament. However, the case has a 'down side' from the perspective of the inherent rights thesis for, with respect to the specific issue addressed here, the court appears to accept the premise that aboriginal sovereignty, if it ever existed, was extinguished by the assertion of sovereignty by Great Britain and Canada.

With regard to the existence of aboriginal rights prior to the establishment of Canada, the court comes out strongly in favour of the inherent right thesis for it asserts that aboriginal rights (in their words on this point, 'Indian title') arises independently of and prior to Canada's coming into being. Thus, the court makes reference to 'the *sui generis* nature of Indian title ...' (p. 24). It also asserts that aboriginal people lived in societies before Canada existed and that this fact forms a basis for identifying aboriginal rights. Thus, they say with respect to an aboriginal right to fish salmon (p. 12): 'The evidence reveals that the Musqueam have lived in the area as an organized society long before the coming of European settlers, and that the taking of salmon was an integral part of their lives and remains so to this day.'

The court's response to extinguishment is more complex. It provides support for the line of reasoning favoured by the attorney-general of Canada cited above with respect to the question of the unilateral extinguishment of sovereignty. Thus, the court asserts (pp. 12–13): 'It is worth recalling that while British policy toward the native population was based on respect for their right to occupy their traditional lands, a proposition to which the Royal Proclamation of 1763 bears witness, *there was from the outset never any doubt that sovereignty and legislative power, and indeed the underlying title, to such lands vest in the Crown*' (emphasis mine). They support this thesis by reference to a leading United States Supreme Court decision, *Johnson v. M'Intosh* (1823), the Royal Proclamation itself, and a leading Canadian Supreme Court decision, *Calder v. Attorney General of British Columbia* (1973). However, they do not support a position that the mere assertion of sovereignty annulled 'existing' aboriginal rights in general. Rather, they argue that such rights, being *sui generis* in nature, continued to exist without the need for special constitutional protection after the Crown asserted sovereignty over the land mass of Canada. In this, they support the argument outlined by Mr. Justice Hall in the Calder case that British law compels the state to make its intent explicit when government legislates with respect to existing rights (Asch 1984). Thus, it suggests from *Calder v. Attorney General of British Columbia* (1973: 16) that: 'The test of extinguishment to be adopted, in our opinion, is that the Sovereign's intention must be clear and plain if it is to extinguish an aboriginal right.'

Following from their reasoning, it is not possible for Canada to assert that acts that 'regulated' rights extinguished them. Rather, the acts had to be explicit. Thus, it is plausible that, in the period prior to the Constitution Act, 1982, the Sovereign's clear and plain intention could be demonstrated through the passage of very specific, but not constitutionally unusual, acts of Parliament. However, at least since the passage of the Constitution Act, 1982 and its express recognition and affirmation of aboriginal and treaty rights, the court greatly constrains the state's ability to act in this area. In fact, it sets out a very specific test for the validity of such legislation. However, it is clear that, if Parliament follows this procedure, it still has the ultimate right to act with respect to aboriginal and treaty rights.

While the court clearly comes down on the side of the Sovereign's right to extinguish, it makes it clear that the 'burden of proving extinguishment' is on the Crown and that, unless the Crown can show that it has extinguished an aboriginal or treaty right clearly and plainly (and, following 1982, in a manner that is constitutionally appropriate), that right continues to exist. This line of reasoning, then, rejects the argument put forward by governments that aboriginal rights do not exist until they have been given effect by legislation or court pronouncement. Since there are very few explicit acts of Parliament or court decisions explicitly respecting the extinguishment, it can be presumed that, speaking broadly, aboriginal rights continue to exist.

What aboriginal rights, then, continue to exist? As a general question, the court is silent on this point, suggesting only that it will determine this matter on a specific-case basis. In this determination, the court notes, the burden of proof will rest with the aboriginal side advocating the aboriginal right. The court, in *Sparrow*, as discussed above, is much more explicit regarding the question of whether aboriginal sovereignty is an existing aboriginal right. It seems to come down strongly in the negative for, to reiterate, the court states: 'There was from the outset never any doubt that sovereignty and legislative power, and indeed the underlying title, to such lands vest(ed) in the Crown.'

It is also true that the *Sparrow* case is not the last word on the subject. Indeed, there are places in other recent Supreme Court decisions that support the idea that aboriginal sovereignty existed at the time of contact and that it was recognized by the Crown. One of these is the remark made by Justice Lemare in the *Siuoi* case to the effect that the British treated aboriginal nations with as much freedom as possible. There are other arguments that could be made. One, for example, could be based on an interpretation of the Royal Proclamation of 1763 which, counter to its use by the court in *Sparrow*, would argue that the proclamation, for example, in the use of the phrase 'hunting grounds' to describe the territory of aboriginal nations, refers to these nations as sovereign bodies and that its intent is to assure these nations that the Crown must first enter into treaty when the colonies wish to expand to their domains (Asch 1989: 218).

To sum up, the Supreme Court has not definitively answered the questions of whether or not an aboriginal right to sovereignty existed in the past; whether or not it was recognized by the Crown; or whether or not it continues to exist, notwithstanding the existence of Canada as a state. The *Sparrow* decision favours an interpretation that suggest that aboriginal rights are *sui generis*, and that they become a burden on the Crown when it becomes sovereign. However, it raises no doubts about that sovereignty and its extension to aboriginal nations. Thus, although there are reasonable interpretations of court decisions and other documents to the contrary, the *Sparrow* decision, which is the most recent, detailed discussion of this topic by the Court, supports the thesis that such a right does not continue to exist.

In light of the above, I think it is fair to conclude that, at minimum, there is nothing definitive in recent Supreme Court decisions to counter the thesis of the attorney-general of Canada that: 'if (any aboriginal nation) ever had sovereignty, it was extinguished completely by the assertion of sovereignty by Great Britain' and to help restrain governments from basing their policies on such a thesis.

CANADIAN STATE POLICY AND ABORIGINAL SOVEREIGNTY

It is therefore not surprising that Canadian policy, at both the federal and provincial levels, has been advanced in a manner consistent with the contingent right thesis. As I understand it, the *Sparrow* decision has resulted in some movement in federal policy away from an approach based primarily on the assumption that aboriginal rights generally do not exist and that, specifically, aboriginal hunting and fishing rights do not need to be dealt with in a careful manner. Indeed, I am informed, this latter point has resulted in certain changes in the proposed agreement-in-principle with the Inuit of the Northwest Territories which are favourable to the aboriginal point of view.

The governments of Canada have remained faithful to the proposition that Canadian state sovereignty 'extinguished' aboriginal sovereignty as an orienting principle in negotiations with aboriginal nations concerning aboriginal self-government. Here are two examples.

First, Canadian governments argued in the First Ministers' Conferences on aboriginal issues that recognition of the legislative authority of aboriginal governments as co-equal to the provinces and the federal government in their areas of jurisdiction would have to await an explicit constitutional amendment to get it into effect. Indeed, the federal government refused to interpret section 91(24) of the Constitution Act, 1867 as an opportunity to assert such recognition independently of the current amending formula which requires passage by seven provinces representing fifty per cent of the population as well as the federal government.

Second, governments have insisted that any self-government agreements with aboriginal nations be based either on the principle of 'delegated authority' (or a form that expressly acknowledges the sovereignty of the provinces and the federal government) or through a form of 'legislative authority,' as in the case of the *Sechelt* legislation (*Sechelt Indian Band Self-Government Act* 1986) which can be unilaterally changed or withdrawn by the federal parliament. It is still, as Sally Weaver points out in a recent paper (1990): 'More generally, by 1990 much remained the same. The Indian Act remained largely in tact. Disagreement over the sources of authority for Indian government continued as the federal position on delegated federal authority remained as firm as the First Nations position on the inherent sovereignty of Indian Nations.'

This position is well illustrated in the 6 February 1990 response of then Minister of Indian and Northern Affairs Pierre Cadieux to a request by Chief Bill Erasmus of the Dene Nation on the topic of self-government negotiations in the context of Dene land claims. The letter gives the Dene the response of the federal cabinet to its review 'regarding the inclusion of self-government agreements in northern land claims settlements ...' (Cadieux 1990). These settlements, of course, represent constitutional documents according to section 35 of the Constitution Act, 1982. Hence, any self-government agreements that were contained with them would automatically receive constitutional recognition.

The Cabinet specifically rejects such an approach. The letter states that, while land claims agreements are protected, '... the separately created self-government institutions would not themselves be constitutionally protected pursuant to Section 35 of the Constitution Act,

1982.' Again, with respect to any self-government arrangements that might be negotiated with the federal or the territorial government, the minister states '... there would not be constitutional protection to the exercise of rights not otherwise provided in claims agreements.' Rather, the Cabinet supports the use of the general amending formula to give effect to aboriginal self-government. The stated rationale for this viewpoint is that 'such an approach will provide an equitable basis for groups everywhere in Canada to receive constitutional protection of negotiated self-government arrangements.' But another rationale is that the Cabinet supports the idea that the aboriginal right to self-government is contingent and hence requires positive action by the state.

Premier Rae of Ontario recently articulated support for an inherent right to aboriginal self-government. He, thus, becomes the first government leader now in power who is prepared to support this point of view. The consensus of government leaders now in power, then, still follows the philosophical orientation that supports the viewpoint on extinguishment and the assertion of sovereignty articulated by the attorney-general of Canada in the case cited above.

DISCUSSION

The above discussion indicates that our constitution acts and court decisions do nothing to authoritatively refute the thesis of the attorney-general of Canada that aboriginal nations may not have had sovereignty at the time of contact and that, even if this were the case, aboriginal sovereignty was extinguished by the mere assertion of sovereignty by Great Britain and, later, Canada. It is especially noteworthy that this thesis finds comfort in the recent *Sparrow* case which, in other respects, represents strong support for the survival of aboriginal rights to the present. It is therefore not surprising that government policy on aboriginal self-government remains consistent with this thesis.

The issue, then, is not the attorney-general made a statement that is inconsistent with our constitutional ideology, but rather that it remains consistent with at least one interpretation of it. The question is how this can be true. The problem, as I see it, is that it seems self-evident that this theory of aboriginal sovereignty and its extinguishment does violence to such universally accepted fundamental principles of justice and human rights in the modern world as the assumed equality of peoples, and especially of their ability to govern themselves, and the basic right of a people to self-determination. These are principles that Canada and Canadians have been proud to advocate on the world stage and especially with respect to the rights of colonized peoples such as Blacks in South Africa. Hence, it is abhorrent that such a theory remains consistent with our own constitutional ideology. Clearly, then, given the accepted standards of world morality and Canada's advocacy of it, the maintenance of such values with respect to Canada itself is contradictory and, in my view, must be changed.

What, then, needs changing? In my view, the key to any thesis regarding aboriginal sovereignty and its extinguishment derives most basically from the set of presuppositions used by Great Britain and later adopted by Canada to assert the legitimate right to self-government over its land mass. As Slattery (1979) points out, there are four principle legal means by which a state can justify the acquisition of new territories. These are by reference to: (1) conquest or the military subjugation of a territory over which the ruler clearly expresses the desire to assume sovereignty on a permanent basis; (2) cession or the formal transfer of a territory (by treaty, for example) from one independent political unit to another; (3) annexation or the assertion of sovereignty over another political entity without military action or treaty; or, (4) the settlement or acquisition of territory that was previously unoccupied or is not recognized as belonging to another political entity.

It is easy to imagine the use of any of these arguments in defence of Canada's claim to the occupation of its territory. It is also clear that the use of the these arguments might well be successful in a legal forum, such as an international court of law. Indeed, I doubt that there would be much support among members of the international community for any such court challenge. Canada is recognized by the world community as being in effective occupation of its territory and, due to the evidence now required to prove a *self-evident* case of colonialism, protected from the practical impact of relevant United Nations declarations on the rights of colonized peoples. However, each of these grounds have certain defects when used as a fundamental orienting principle for constitutional identity with respect to aboriginal sovereignty (for an alternative approach to this material see Davies 1958).

One approach, conquest, was roundly and convincingly condemned by Bill Wilson, an aboriginal leader from British Columbia, when he stated at the first First Ministers' Conference on aboriginal issues (quoted in Asch 1984: 29): 'When the German forces occupied France, did the French people believe they didn't own the country? I sincerely doubt that there was a French person in France during the war that ever had the belief that France belonged to Germany, which is why, of course, they struggled with our assistance to liberate their country and once again take it back for themselves.' A similar logic applies to the annexation position. It is an argument that suggests that, especially in the postcolonial world, the legitimacy of a new sovereign over a conquered or annexed territory derives less from the standing of the aggressor than from the will of the victims of that aggression.

The two other justifications for the acquisition of new territories are more specifically applicable to Canada's view of its own case. Below, I will discuss the 'cession' thesis. First, I will discuss the settlement thesis for it is clear that this is the theory that provides support for the assertion of the attorney-general regarding aboriginal sovereignty and its extinguishment the assertion of sovereignty by Great Britain.

The settlement thesis is perfectly justifiable, even within contemporary ideology, in one case: where there really were no previous occupants of the land. The justification becomes troublesome only in the situation where the assertion is made in the face of evidence of human occupation contemporaneous with the first assertion of sovereignty. In this case, the justification must be transformed into an argument about the nature of the population that occupied the land base and its attributes, in particular, with respect to indigenous sovereignty and its survival.

I am aware of at least four arguments that are brought forward to justify the assertion of settlement in the face of contemporaneous occupation by another population. One of these, to my knowledge, is unique to a particular situation. It is the argument put forth by Israel that it is the Jewish population that is truly the earlier occupants and those others who happened to live in the land base of Israel at the time of the assertion of Israeli sovereignty are the later arrivals. The second argument is that there are no original people; that, rather, all are immigrants. This is the type of argument I have heard mounted in the United States of America with respect to the assertion of special rights on the part of aboriginal nations. However, this is undoubtedly a secondary argument within American state ideology. The primary ideology, which flows from the concept of 'domestic dependent nation' developed by the Supreme Court of the United States under Chief Justice Marshall, is that of conquest. And it is subject to the type of criticism exemplified in Bill Wilson's remarks cited above.

The third, which I have heard most frequently in the context of Mexico and Latin America, asserts that the settlement thesis is legit-imate but that everyone in the state is 'aboriginal.' This thesis is based on assumptions such as the idea that, through intermarriage and other institutions, there has been a true integration of the descen-dants of the aboriginal people and of the colonists into a single society. Therefore, the state represents a single people that is the outcome of the combination of cultures and biology. I am uncertain of the status of this thesis within Latin American constitutional ideol-ogy. However, I doubt if it is significant within the context of consti-tutional documents and court interpretations. I would guess that other ideas, such as the one discussed below, as well as the conquest thesis play a more significant role. Let me hasten to add that this thesis could well be reasonable and, indeed, fit within the cession thesis as I will outline it below, were it factually correct. But it is not. Despite intermarriage and the reshaping of indigenous institutions through the impact of colonialism, aboriginal collectivities exist today that still see themselves as autonomous from the national culture and polity.

The fourth is the version that is the most typical of colonial regimes, especially in pre-Second World War Africa and Asia. Specifically, this version asserts the settlers were superior to the original inhabitants, especially with respect to something akin to political sovereignty. Hence, the land base, when examined with respect to competing claims of the settlers and the original inhabitants, must be more ap-propriately in the hands of the former. Styles of this version began with colonial expansion and included such particulars as (Asch 1984): the superiority of Christianity over heathen religions; of agriculture over hunting and gathering; of western cultural institutions such as private property over non-western ones; and, of course, of one skin colour over another. It is precisely this latter version of the settlement thesis that lies behind the remarks of the attorney-general, for it is only when it is framed from the perspective on the inherent superior-ity of British and Canadian society that one can make logical sense of the remark that 'If the Plaintiff ever had sovereignty, it was extin-guished completely by the assertion of sovereignty by Great Britain.' No other interpretative framework used to justify the acquisition of new territories by a sovereign can make sense of this remark.

The cession thesis represents the final means by which a state can legally justify the acquisition of new territories. This thesis is based on the presumption of a formal transfer of sovereignty from one power to another, as through a treaty. Cession ranks as an important legal justification for Canadian sovereignty, but, as I will outline below, it is still subordinate to the settlement thesis in constitutional ideology. In support of the cession thesis, Canada can point to the existence of treaties (such as the numbered treaties on the Plains), and especially to their written versions. Of particular importance here, of course, is the clause, found in all post-Confederation treaties, that conveys the idea, as found in the words of Treaty Number Four that (quoted in Asch 1984: 116): '[the said] Indians ... *cede*, release, surrender and yield up to the Government of the Dominion of Canada, for Her Majesty the Queen, and Her successors forever, all their rights, titles and privileges whatsoever, to the lands included ...' Thus, it is not hard to imagine that, were Canada to be met with a court challenge on sovereignty within a treaty area, the attorney-general might well use the argument of cession rather than that of settlement as was employed in the Gitksan case.

Were these treaties formal cessions as they appear to be in their written versions, Canada's argument regarding legitimacy might gain stature, at least in those regions covered by treaty. But, in fact, do the treaties represent formal cessions, based on the free will of the aboriginal nations, that cede unilateral sovereignty to the Crown? That is, are the written versions of the treaties factually accurate? There are strong doubts. In the first place, aboriginal nations from all over Canada argue that the written versions are not accurate; that, in fact, treaties were produced for peace and friendship and to allow for peaceful settlement of non-natives on aboriginal lands and/or to form a political relationship between two sovereigns, but were never considered to provide unilateral cessions of sovereignty. The possibility that the written versions of treaties are not accurate reflections of the negotiations is supported by the Supreme Court which has suggested, for example, in *Siuoi* that, where the language of the treaty is ambiguous, the assessment of the benefit of the doubt must favour the aboriginal interpretation. As well in the *Paulette* case, where the trial judge was able to hear aboriginal signatories to a treaty first hand, doubts were expressed as to the accuracy of the specific and unambiguous clause that ceded the lands to Canada.

What is the importance of the cession thesis in our constitutional ideology? If cession were the dominant theme, then, Canada would act differently with regard to aboriginal nations in at least one respect: it would ensure that treaties were made before it asserted sovereignty in any new territory. Thus, in the case cited in the attorney-general's remarks, Canada would be actively seeking to negotiate with the Gitksan rather than defend itself in litigation through the use of the settlement theory's presumption of the Sovereign's unilateral right to extinguish aboriginal sovereignty. Equally, the federal government would not limit its language on self-government in comprehensive land claims agreements to that found in section 7.1.5 of the Dene–Metis Final Agreement (1990) which states that 'Nothing in this agreement is intended to affect any aboriginal or treaty right to self-government which the Dene/Metis *may have.*' Rather, Canada would accept the continued existence of such self-government until cession had taken place. Finally, if cession were a primary aspect for justification, our constitution would likely express this fact in its ideology. It is, thus, apparent that the settlement thesis forms the basis for our constitutional ideology even where presumed cessions have already taken place.

CONCLUSIONS

Clearly, the colonialist version of the settlement thesis lies at the heart of our constitutional identity with respect to the justification of our occupation of the land mass of Canada in the face of aboriginal claims to self-determination and self-government. This is the reason for my assertion that Canadian constitutional ideology structurally implies premises that are racist and colonial. How, then, did Canada arrive at this unfortunate situation? Clearly, there are a number of answers that range from self-serving political interests of politicians bent on maintaining the status quo and historical traditions, to fears of accepting any alternatives and underlying ideological premises. Here, I wish to focus only on the latter two: fears and ideological premises. I begin with the latter.

I have argued that our current ideological premise is universalism. This thesis, as Smith (1969) points out, produces an inexorable force toward the assimilation of minorities into the culture of the majority. The question is how this is achieved. A measure of the answer lies in the very way universalism models the relationship between the state and its citizens. Because this thesis focuses on the presupposition that the state must only see individuals and, within that context, see each individual as structurally equal (or identical), state ideology does not expressly recognize the possible existence of cultural difference within its population. Thus, where there are minority and majority cultures coexisting within a state, state institutions, because they do not recognize cultural difference, become unconsciously structured around the cultural values of the majority. Hence, they generate the assimilative tendency.

The recognition of a pre-existing political society conflicts with universalism in that it supports the existence of a structurally separate community within an ideology that will not accept any community other than that composed of equal individuals who make up the people. The fact that the pre-existing political society to be recognized is a minority population within the state only heightens the contradiction, for it undermines the legitimacy of the assimilative tendency of state institutions. Better, if one is bound by universalism, to support 'majority rule,' than inherent rights of minority peoples.

The settlement thesis, then, especially in its colonialist form, fits neatly with universalistic ideology. Universalism suggests that the majority is the collective of equal individuals who make up the population of the state. Within this framework, aboriginal peoples, rather than being conceptualized as a unique collective segment of society, become considered as merely one small component of the total population, one that is required, like the others, to accept the domination of the institutions of the majority population. Such a thesis is legitimate to the extent that the majority as it is defined by universalism is legitimate. This is where the thesis of settlement is important. Were aboriginal sovereignty non-existent or, at least, extinguished by the mere assertion of sovereignty by Great Britain and, later, Canada, then history begins with contact. Thus, as no one can claim 'prior' status, the legitimate majority becomes the majority that evolved after contact, and the legitimate constitutional as well as general history of Canada becomes the constitutional and general history of this majority. Hence, the settlement thesis, which is itself colonialist in nature, becomes an important foundation for the ideology of universalism which, as it is often expressed, strongly disavows such concepts.

The alternative thesis, which I would advocate, would begin by accepting the premise that aboriginal nations were sovereign at the time of contact and that their sovereignty remains unextinguished until it is changed by mutual consent. This thesis assumes that any transformation of sovereign status is based on negotiations and probably finds its language through a treaty between nations. In this sense, the position I advocate follows most closely the cession thesis. Indeed, I would accept as valid the aboriginal point of view that the treaties were about peace and friendship and/or mutual intertwining of sovereignties and work to develop further negotiated relations that would eventually lead to forms of confederation, where these did not already exist (as through previous treaties). It is an approach that would be based on the concept of direct consociation. However, I also believe that many Canadians will avoid advocacy of this point of view because they would fear that it might lead to the delegitimization of Canadian sovereignty. In this, I think they are wrong. Aboriginal nations have repeatedly asserted that their goal is to achieve recognition of their sovereignty and not to overturn the sovereignty of the Canadian state. This may be for philosophical or for practical reasons; it is nonetheless the case. Indeed, it is made clear that aboriginal nations, like the Dene, seek, as the 1975 Dene Declaration suggests (Asch 1984: 128): 'Independence and self-determination within Canada. This is what we mean when we call for a just land settlement for the Dene Nation.' In short, aboriginal peoples are looking for means to enter into, not destroy, confederation. It is a proposition that at this time in Canada's constitutional history needs to be fostered.

Acknowledgments

I wish to thank Michael Levin, Patrick Macklem, Peter Meekison, Richard Price, Brian Slattery, and Sharon Venne for their helpful comments on various drafts on this paper and to acknowledge the financial support of the Anthropology Committee of SSHRCC which provided research funds used in the preparation of this paper. Many of the ideas presented in this paper are updated and explored at greater length in a paper entitled 'Aboriginal Self-Government and the Construction of Canadian Constitutional Identity' which was published in *The Alberta Law Review* (1992), 30(2): 465–91.

REFERENCES

Asch, Michael. 1990. 'Consociation and the Resolution of Aboriginal Political Rights: The Example of the Northwest Territories, Canada.' *Culture* 10(1): 92–102
– 1989. 'Defining the Animals the Dene Hunt and the Settlement of Aboriginal Rights Claims.' *Canadian Public Policy* 15: 205–19
– 1984. *Home and Native Land: Aboriginal Rights and the Canadian Constitution*. Toronto: Methuen
Attorney-General of Canada. 1989. 'Statement of the Attorney-General of

Canada's Position on Extinguishment, Diminution or Abandonment of Aboriginal Rights in the Claim Area of the Gitksan–Wet'suwet'en, December 11, 1989. Unpublished Document

Cadieux, Pierre H., Minister of Indian and Northern Affairs. 1990. Letter to Mr. Bill Erasmus, President, Dene Nation. Dated 6 February 1990

Calder v. Attorney General of British Columbia. 1973. 34 *Dominion Law Review* (3D) 145 (S.C.C.)

Connor, Walker. 1973. 'The Politics of Ethnonationalism.' *Journal of International Affairs* 27(1): 1–21

Dene/Metis Final Agreement. 1990. Government of Canada: Department of Indian and Northern Affairs

Davies, Maureen. 1985. 'Aspects of Aboriginal Rights in International Law,' in B. Morse (ed.), *Aboriginal Peoples and the Law: Indian, Metis and Inuit Rights in Canada.* Ottawa: Carleton Library Series, pp. 16–47

Johnson v. M'Intosh. 1823. 21 U.S. (8 Wheat.) 543 (1823)

Lijphart, A. 1977. *Democracy in Plural Societies: A Comparative Exploration.* New Haven: Yale University Press

R. v. Horseman. 1990. 4 W.W.R. 97 (S.C.C.)

R. v. Sioui. 1990. 70 D.L.R. (4th) 427 (S.C.C.)

R. v. Sparrow. 1990. 70 D.L.R. (4th) 385 (S.C.C.)

Rae, Bob 1990. 'Transcript of Remarks by Premier Bob Rae to the Assembly of First Nations Banquet, University of Toronto, Tuesday, October 2, 1990.' (unpublished manuscript)

Re: Paulette's Application [1973] 6 W.W.R. 97 (N.W.T.S.C.)

Sechelt Indian Band Self-Government Act. 1986. S.C. 1986, c. 27

Slattery, Brian. 1979. The Land Rights of Indigenous Canadian Peoples, as Affected by the Crown's Acquisition of Their Territory. Unpublished D.Phil. Dissertation, Oxford University

Smith, M.G. 1969. 'Some Developments in the Analytic Framework of Pluralism,' in L. Kuper and M.G. Smith (eds.), *Pluralism in Africa.* Berkeley: University of California Press, pp. 415–58

Van Dyke, B. 1980. 'The Cultural Rights of Peoples.' *Universal Human Rights Journal* 2(2):1

Van Loon, R., and M. Whittington. 1987. *The Canadian Political System: Environment, Structure and Process,* 4th ed. Toronto: McGraw-Hill Ryerson

Weaver, Sally. 1990. 'Self-Government Policy for Indians, 1980–1990: Political Transformation or Symbolic Gestures.' Unpublished paper (revised 25 July 1990) delivered to UNESCO Conference on 'Migration and the Transformation of Cultures in Canada,' Calgary, Alberta, 21–2 October 1989

CHAPTER 3

Self-Determination, National Pressure Groups, and Australian Aborigines: The National Aboriginal Conference 1983–1985

Sally M. Weaver

After World War I, when the idea of 'the self-determination of nations' was popularized by President Woodrow Wilson of the United States, indigenous peoples in Western democracies tried to establish national political organizations to promote their interests to their respective nation-states. But it was not until the post-World War II period that the nationalistic movements of 'Fourth World' peoples took firmer hold. The movements rejected the historical control by the colonizing agencies and, under the banner of self-determination, sought the power and freedom to define themselves as distinct peoples – culturally different from the immigrant societies that surrounded them – and to shape the political institutions best suited, in their eyes, to promoting their interests.

Self-determination was a broadly conceived notion much in keeping with the United Nations definition of it as the right of peoples 'to freely determine their political status and freely pursue their economic, social and cultural development.'[1] In subsequent years the concept of self-determination remained as fuzzy and poorly defined as the related idea of nationalism. Whether construed as a collective movement to enhance *cultural* autonomy or a collective force to promote *political* autonomy (see Wolf 1986: 103; Long and Boldt 1988: 112), Fourth World nationalism invariably sought both forms of freedom. Often, the movements in the different countries began with demands for cultural recognition and autonomy, and then, reflecting the growing political self-awareness of the indigenous peoples, the focus shifted to political autonomy, the units of political independence often characterized as nations or tribes. Thus, for example, in Canada an early spokesman for the Indian movement stressed that an Indian nation was to be given a cultural interpretation as a spiritual–traditional entity, not a political meaning as Quebec was seeking (Cardinal 1977: 141). Soon, however, other indigenous leaders began using nation in a political sense. Thus, the Dene of northern Canada demanded recognition of their Dene Nation (Erasmus 1977: 179) and insisted on 'the right to define, protect and present our own interest' (Dene Nation 1977: 182). With time and experience, self-determination was linked more forcefully and explicitly by indigenous peoples to demands for political rights and powers. The Assembly of First Nations (AFN), the national organ for Canadian Indians, was, for example, very clear about how it interpreted this linkage: 'For the First Nations self-determination goes much beyond entitlement to practise our own cultures, traditional customs, religions and languages, or the right to determine the development of our own identity. Self-determination includes constitutionally-protected powers over our lives, our lands and our resources as well as the right to determine the nature of our on-going relationships with the federal and provincial governments within Canada' (AFN 1986: 24). The AFN's perspective reflected the distinction between cultural and political nationalism (see also, e.g., Kienetz 1988: 11). But the AFN set aside this distinction as the political component was seen to subsume the cultural aspects.

The concept of nationalism is a highly controversial one in the literature (e.g., Riggs 1986; White 1985). For this essay I have adopted Connor's approach largely because it is compatible with the empirical data. Connor defines nationalism as 'the tendency of peoples to perceive human relations from the vantage point of the ethnic group and to demand that political institutions and borders be made to conform with the best interests of the ethnic group' (1973: 2).

Nationalistic movements can be very powerful vehicles for political change. When these movements took form among Fourth World peoples, their goals were often to create new political structures and resources to serve the needs and hopes of the indigenous peoples and to forge a new relationship with the nation-states in which they lived. In short, they sought to establish a new political regime, one in which they were the architects of their own institutions. They were unlikely to form independent sovereign states, but short of that, they could be expected to establish their own political organs in the democratic context in which they existed.

The national political organizations of Fourth World peoples that originated in the 1960s and early 1970s were an integral part of these nationalistic movements. Demands by indigenous peoples for political change did not stop at the local and regional levels. Emerging native spokesmen, often younger and more educated than their predecessors, saw the need for national organizations to represent their interests to the nation-state because policies emanated from the national level, policies they were determined to influence. In the face of enormous odds, including political inexperience, tribal/local diversity, and poverty, the spokesmen began to promote a national identity and political unity, in part by establishing national pressure groups. As vehicles to define and deliver their interests to the policy authorities, these organs were, at the same time, products of, and contributors to, growing nationalism, much as Sawchuk (1978) noted for the Manitoba Métis Federation in Canada.

By the 1980s, however, the first generation of national organizations was found wanting by both the Fourth World peoples and the nation-states. Democratic governments, seeking representative advice and unity of opinion, found little policy coherence or political cohesion in these organizations. And politically astute indigenous leaders, frustrated with their limited influence, recognized the need for grass-roots strength in their organizations if they hoped to affect the policy process. As vehicles for transmitting policy ideas between governments and indigenous constituents, the national organizations had performed ineffectually the key functions of pressure groups – political communication, conferring policy legitimacy, and administration (Pross 1986: 87). To correct these organizational weaknesses, reform measures were attempted in the 1980s that gave birth to a new generation of national political bodies.[2]

If self-determination means anything in the *realpolitik* of the Fourth World, the notion should include the right of indigenous peoples to devise and maintain their own political organizations to advocate their special interests to the nation-state. And this right should apply whether these organizations be local, regional, national, or sectoral (e.g., education, legal aid, housing). The literature on Fourth World nationalism has focused on significant topics such as identity formation (e.g., Beckett 1988), land claims (e.g., Kienetz 1986), and northern hemisphere constitutional developments (e.g., Elliott 1984; Kienetz 1987). But the relationship between self-determination, national pressure groups, and the nation-state has received very little attention.

This paper presents one case study of national organizational reform in the 1980s, and it asks to what extent these particular Fourth World peoples were able to design and establish their own reform organizations – in short, to what extent was self-determination actually applied to this case of organizational reform. The case examines the role of Aboriginals in the attempted reorganization of the Australian National Aboriginal Conference in the 1983–85 period. Following the case description, I will conclude by identifying the key factors which fostered and then impeded organizational self-determination at the national level in Australia.

AUSTRALIA: NATIONAL ABORIGINAL CONFERENCE
REFORM 1983–5

Aboriginal Australians had formed local and regional organizations before World War II, but it was not until 1967, when the national (federal) government in Canberra gained concurrent legislative powers over Aborigines with the state governments, that a focus existed in government for Aboriginal pressure. In 1972 the newly elected Labor government launched many social policy reforms. In Aboriginal Affairs, it appointed the first minister to head the first Department of Aboriginal Affairs (DAA), and he created the first national Aboriginal organization, the National Aboriginal Consultative Council (NACC), as a policy advising body to the minister. The NACC, a body of forty-one nationally elected Aborigines, was a response to the long-held desire by Aboriginal activists and white supporters for a 'truly representative' national Aboriginal body to influence policy in Canberra. But the government withdrew its commitment to the NACC even before it was operative and cut off funding at one point to curtail its confrontational behaviour. The NACC sought more than advisory powers, but was unable to provide reliable policy advice to the government or settle its own internal conflicts.

In 1976, the new Liberal government (1975–83) overrode a report it commissioned on the NACC by anthropologist Les Hiatt (see Hiatt 1976). On the basis of nation-wide consultations with Aborigines, Hiatt had recommended the reform of the NACC into a larger, stronger, government-funded pressure group. But Viner, the new minister of Aboriginal Affairs, wanted a more manageable advisory body under his authority (Weaver 1983). Consequently he abolished the NACC in 1976 and established the National Aboriginal Conference (NAC), a smaller, weaker 'consultative body' designed by DAA officials (public servants) and officially approved as policy by the federal cabinet (Viner 1977).

From its birth in the November 1977 election, the thirty-five-member NAC predictably encountered severe problems of legitimacy with the Aboriginal public and the government. Unlike the radical NACC, the NAC was politically passive in its first term of office (1977–81), gaining a reputation as 'a lightweight and conservative body' that 'lacked credibility.'[3] The 1981 NAC election, however, recruited a few younger, more politically sensitive members who began to speak out more critically on Aboriginal issues, but their increased activity only highlighted the NAC's difficulties. By the end of the Liberal government (April 1983), the NAC was starved for adequate resources, in terms both of finances and personnel, and some of its executive and staff members were deeply worried about its future.

The NAC's problems on the eve of reform efforts in 1983 were pervasive. Briefly, although the NAC was a creature of government, it had not created for itself a collective sense of purpose, either operationally or politically. There was no articulation of the role of the NAC with emerging Aboriginal political ideology, and no identification of Aborigines with the NAC as their own organization.

Second, the NAC had not developed a policy capacity. It had no collective understanding of what policy was and, with the exception of the few educated young activists in both the executive and secretariat (the administrative wing of the organization), no understanding of how policy related to grass-roots demands and needs. There was no clear view of how Aboriginal-based policy could be devised within the NAC, and little comprehension of how the NAC could deliver its positions to government and the media in a compelling manner. As a result, the NAC neither responded to the minister's requests for advice (few though these requests were), nor initiated its own policy proposals to government that reflected Aboriginal concerns.

Third was the related problem of leadership at both the political and administrative levels of the organization. The executive dwelt on administrative matters, factional conflicts, and personality disputes, and its activities of hiring and firing staff were deeply intrusive in the operations of the secretariat. The executive was unable to provide political leadership despite some genuine attempts by successive national chairmen to bring some discipline and focus to the group. The secretariat, comprised of twelve persons (1982), was understaffed, underfunded, and undersupervised, and its personnel became politicized by factional alignments in the executive. The executive's practice of keeping the secretary-general, the top administrative post, on short-term contracts made him even more vulnerable to the political whims of the executive. The more educated staff were highly critical of this political intervention, but when they tried to direct the executive's attention to policy matters, through policy option briefs, the staff were reprimanded by the less secure or less educated executive members for usurping their political-policy role.

Fourth, from the outset, the NAC had been chronically underfunded by the government, limiting its capacity to initiate action and to respond to Aboriginal constituents' concerns. Equally significant was the NAC's dependence on several government departments for its resources. The NAC was firmly locked into the government's annual budget cycle, its accounting procedures and priorities, and its personnel systems – including job classifications and hiring procedures. For legal advice, transportation, salaries, office equipment, and conducting its own elections, the NAC was required to use different bureaucratic agencies in the federal government. The NAC thus became an administrative appendage of government, subject to government standards, timetables, and priorities, and government views of NAC needs.

Fifth, the political role of the individual NAC members was purposely vague in the NAC's charter. The NAC did not subsequently develop the perceived need to maintain close and continuous contact with local communities. Consequently, the NAC's ability to obtain the views of local constituents and to report back to them on its work was severely limited. The NAC's publication program did not value quick and responsive newsletters or videos to inform the Aboriginal public of its activities. This failure in political communication led to accusations that the NAC was unaccountable, unrepresentative, and inactive.

Sixth, the NAC collectively had not developed a clear sense of where it fit into the total scheme of national Aboriginal organs in Australia. The national field of Aboriginal politics contained not only the government-created NAC, but Aboriginal-created specialized associations formed in the early 1970s to provide various services to Aborigines (e.g., medical aid and legal aid). The field also contained government-created organs to address specific Aboriginal needs (e.g., Land Councils to administer Aboriginal lands secured under the Aboriginal Land Rights (Northern Territory) Act 1976, and the Aboriginal Development Commission created in 1980 to promote economic development). Intergroup relations among these bodies were often characterized by conflict, competition, and distrust, and their collective advice to government was at times contradictory.

Finally, the NAC's relations with government were not effective in promoting Aboriginal interests. With the exception of the younger, educated Aboriginal staff and members, the NAC had no operational knowledge of government on which to base effective intervention in the policy process. Generally, relations with the DAA were a mixture of dependency and distrust. While some DAA officials had been sympathetic and supportive of the NAC over the years, others, including the leading Aboriginal bureaucrat in Canberra, Charles Perkins, were contemptuous of its various incapacities.[4] Decidedly, the NAC was not a threat to the bureaucracy either in terms of persuasive policy positions, mobilization of Aboriginal activism, or strategic use of pressure points within government to exact concessions.

The idea of reforming the NAC was couched in terms of Aboriginal self-determination from the outset. The notion of reform, however, originated not in the NAC, but from official campaign policy of the Australian Labor Party (ALP). When the ALP gained power in the March 1983 federal election under Prime Minister Bob Hawke, Clyde Holding was appointed Minister of Aboriginal Affairs, and the stage was set for NAC reform. Under ALP policy the NAC was to be 'strengthened and restructured' in consultation with the NAC members and other Aboriginal bodies so it could 'extend its powers as a policy making organizing authority [sic] among Aboriginal and Islander communities' (ALP 1982: 6). Consultation would make a reorganized NAC 'a more culturally appropriate national body to advise government,' and adequate funding would allow it to perform its job responsibly, thereby implementing the key principle in Aboriginal policy, 'self-determination' (undefined) (ALP 1983: 25).

Clyde Holding was a long-time supporter of Aboriginal causes and he enthusiastically embraced the policy, actively encouraging the NAC to reform itself into a respected, powerful voice for the some 180,000 Aboriginal Australians. His early months in power were heady times of high expectations for changes in many aspects of the portfolio. Holding's distrust of the bureaucracy, common in the Labour Party, was felt sharply by the DAA, and his preference for Aboriginal policy advice was publicly known. Indeed, in his first meeting with the NAC executive, in mid-March 1983, Holding virtually told the NAC it would be formulating policy: he wanted the NAC to regard him 'not so much as Minister but as a working partner' for his job, and that the DAA, was 'to enable the policies which you yourselves formulate to be advanced as progressively and as quickly as possible within the various areas of government.'[5] Initially, under ALP policy, the DAA was to assist the NAC in this regard, in keeping with wider reforms in the portfolio to promote Aboriginal input into the policy process. And the other national bodies established by Aboriginals were to be upgraded financially and expected to provide 'specialized' policy advice to Holding.

To convey his sincerity to improve the NAC through reform, Holding offered it extraordinary opportunities and resources. He gave the NAC ministerial recognition as his principle advisory body, and he assigned it a pivotal policy function, that of advising him on the formulation of new national land rights legislation – the policy flagship in the portfolio. NAC endorsement of his land rights proposals was requisite, he stressed, before he would carry them to cabinet for approval. At the NAC's request, he provided unique access to himself on a daily basis by placing a NAC member in his ministerial office, an exceedingly rare opportunity to exert policy influence. Holding directed the DAA to secure NAC opinion on bureaucratic advice to him, a step understandably unpopular within the department. Following the NAC's budget submission, he doubled its annual budget from $3.7 million (Australian dollars) in 1982–3, to $7.3 million in 1983–4. He agreed to a major personnel increase in staff positions in the NAC's secretariat for 1983–4. Also at the NAC's request, he funded a July 1983 workshop for NAC members to develop an approach to restructuring the NAC. And, finally, he financed the NAC's selection of lawyers to provide the NAC with legal advice independently of government on the formulation of the new land rights policy.

In addition to recognition and resources, Holding made known his goals for the NAC in his ministry. Generally, he envisaged the NAC becoming an 'umbrella' organization (peak pressure group) for all Aboriginal groups, like the national labour federation he was familiar with, and he urged the NAC to develop a sound foundation in Aboriginal communities so it could speak confidently on Aboriginal issues. He hoped the NAC would become 'recognized by governments and the Australian community as the authoritative, unified voice of Aboriginal people' (*Aboriginal Newsletter* 1983b: 4). On the relevance of 'self-determination' to political organizations he was equally direct: 'The government believes in Aboriginal self-determination and that means Aboriginal organizations have got to not merely formulate policy, but take responsibility for the policy decisions which they formulate' (*Aboriginal Newsletter* 1983a: 1). In the end, Holding wanted a reliable and respected NAC as an instrumental goal to provide policy legitimation for his land rights legislation – without Aboriginal support he expected difficulties in cabinet and among the public.

The NAC's initial reaction to Holding's reform initiative was a mixture of disbelief that the Liberal era of financial drought and political disregard was over (*NAC News* 1984) and a sense of euphoria over promised resources and special status in the eyes of the new government. Even DAA officials, in the words of the NAC's secretary-general, were 'bending over backwards' to help the NAC cope with the changes. At the outset, there was firm insistence from the NAC's secretariat that the NAC must initiate any recommendations for reforming itself. Detailed strategy for dealing with Holding and for planning the July workshop was undertaken by the NAC's research director. In a sophisticated briefing to the NAC's executive,[6] the research director argued that the NAC's crucial need was to find a clear role for itself locally and nationally and then to formulate a more detailed scheme of 'how we see the structure of the NAC.' He believed the ALP policy on NAC reform offered 'the greatest opportunity for the NAC to become a strong political force in Aboriginal Affairs,' but clear purposeful action would be needed from the Aboriginal people if this were to eventuate. In a most prophetic statement, however, he warned the executive that 'the danger is that the NAC may "self-destruct" by simply being unable to perform at the higher level required by the Government or by an expectant Aboriginal community.' In the position paper he prepared for the July workshop on NAC reform, the research director went on to propose that the NAC become an independent, responsible pressure group ('political lobby') that worked cooperatively with other national Aboriginal organizations and that initiated policies from its grassroots constituents.[7] He stressed that its advice would go directly to the minister, not indirectly through the DAA, where, in the NAC's experience, it was screened and sometimes distorted. However, the strong desire to reform the NAC that emanated from the NAC's research staff was repeatedly rebuffed by the NAC's executive.

Not surprisingly, the July workshop failed to raise any interest in collective self-appraisal. Some NAC members explained that few in the NAC had the political sophistication to appreciate the need for organizational reform, while others credited the failure to the Aboriginal consultants who ran the sessions. The basic reason, however, was that the NAC, more particularly its executive, was sharply divided into two camps on the question of reform. The pro-reform faction linked Western Australia and the Northern Territory members. Headed by Rob Riley, a Perth-based executive member, this western alignment sought reform of the NAC into a 'political lobby' by developing strong ties to the grass roots for legitimacy, by forging policy in cooperation with the other national specialized bodies including the Federation of Land Councils, and by strengthening the policy research capacity of the secretariat. They sought a national perspective for the NAC and were far more sympathetic to policies that were sensitive to traditional Aboriginal communities.

In contrast, the status quo faction linked Queensland and New South Wales members, the more urbanized wing of the Aboriginal movement. Headed by Ray Robinson, from Queensland, this alignment believed the NAC needed resources, not restructuring. They stressed the NAC's status as the pre-eminent advisory body to the minister and had a frame of reference oriented to the government rather than the Aboriginal community. They tended to see the NAC as a resource to serve regional (state) rather than national Aboriginal interests, and they often questioned the need to seek Aboriginal views, arguing that these were secured during the NAC election campaigns every three years. Unlike the pro-reform faction that was linked to the Land Councils, this alignment was linked to the Aboriginal Legal Services and other eastern-based organizations, and sought to 'control' these other organizations rather than cooperate with them on policy initiatives. Also unlike the pro-reform faction that wanted a NAC election called in the hope of recruiting new members that were reform-minded and grass-roots oriented, this faction pressed Holding to *extend* the current members' three-year term of office and sought time to let the newly promised resources show results. Policy development was not emphasized as an organizational priority at the national level, in part because this eastern-based faction was not nationally oriented, but also in part because Queensland had held some very effective policy workshops at the state level (Randell and Shelley 1983) under the leadership of the Queensland's state branch chairman, Steve Mam. With some justification this success was cited as proof that the current structure was workable, especially at the state level, if properly funded. The government's initiative to reform the NAC had simply reinforced these previously existing alignments within the NAC. However, with the Queensland faction in power, the executive rejected reform, and continued to dismiss the need to seek local Aboriginal views.

The self-reform phase of organizational reform ended abruptly in early September 1983, six months after Holding had initiated it. Openly impatient with the NAC's inability to see its weaknesses and anxious to begin drafting a new land rights legislation, Holding appointed Dr 'Nugget' Coombs, a former adviser to prime ministers on Aboriginal Affairs, to examine the NAC and report by Christmas on how it might be effectively reorganized. Holding liked the idea of a nationally elected body and wanted Coombs to examine the NAC's electoral boundaries, long recognized as requiring change. But Coombs felt this could pre-empt his findings, so he proceeded to consult Aboriginals to the extent the limited time allowed. He submitted his 'Draft' preliminary report to Holding by mid-December 1983 (Coombs 1983) and circulated confidential copies to the NAC and academics for comment in January 1984.

Coombs's recommendations were for a powerful, well-resourced national body, operating independently of the DAA. It was to provide Aboriginal policy advice directly to the government, not indirectly through the bureaucracy, which he distrusted. Coombs's proposal for a powerful body lay in his firm belief that Aboriginals should have such bodies and in his assessment that Holding was sincere in his desire for a strong NAC in the context of self-determination. Although Coombs had not thought through the meaning of self-determination, it implied to him 'some form of power sharing' with Aboriginals in which the NAC would become 'an executive body' in formulating policy: He stressed that 'At that stage I didn't have any clear notion of what power, but I certainly had a conviction that the NAC was powerless.'[8] Coombs wanted to do the review, having enjoyed a similar experience working recently with the Aboriginal land council based in Alice Springs. But he believed Aboriginals should shape their own institutions if they were to identify with them. Coombs wanted the NAC to regard his review as a tool the NAC could use to reform itself. As his research assistant observed, 'He wanted to hand the review to the NAC on a platter,' but the executive neither perceived his intent nor felt reform was needed. The executive was not asked if it wanted an externally based review, and its members were understandably threatened by Coombs's appointment. Led by the Queensland faction, the executive effectively boycotted the review at the beginning. When Coombs continued his work and reported his preliminary findings to the executive in November 1983, hostility

toward him sharpened. His findings showed that the NAC was neither communicating effectively with Aboriginal communities or
organizations, nor performing its new role as primary policy adviser
to the government. By this point his criticism of the NAC had been
joined by others.

Rob Riley, head of the NAC's reform faction, resigned from the
executive in November, citing publicly the executive's lack of 'a sense
of common purpose' as his main reason. But privately he delivered
a stinging attack on the executive before leaving,[9] claiming it was
unskilled in its approach to major policy issues, such as land claims,
and self-serving in its use of the NAC as 'a private mealticket.' Riley
said Holding had given the NAC 'unprecedented responsibilities' and
a chance to show it could represent Aboriginal people fairly on
issues. Instead of responding responsibly, it focused on 'piddly issues
and ... personalities' and persisted in its 'top dog' superior attitude
toward Aboriginal people. Arguing that the NAC should not be surprised at Coombs's criticisms of it, he said, 'we have lost touch with
ordinary people. We lack solidarity within our own organization and
we lack a basic understanding of what we're about.' The NAC gave
him 'the impression of an organization set on self-destruct' and he
felt it would stay doomed unless it was 'able and willing to grow up
and start acting with maturity and in harmony with other Aboriginal
organizations.' While members of Riley's reform alignment were not
above benefitting from the new-found resources of the NAC, their
observations of the NAC's difficulties had much substance.

In addition to these political problems, financial management
problems were now overtaking the NAC, in part because the secretariat lacked adequately trained personnel in this field, in part
because the DAA did not move supportively from the outset to provide assistance, and in part because the NAC hired new staff before
Holding's promised personnel increases materialized. A few DAA
officials were temporarily assigned to the NAC in September to help
it cope, but by Christmastime the NAC was in severe difficulty. In
fact, six months previously (July 1983) the NAC's annual audit had
failed to pass normal accounting standards, but the executive had
taken no action on the matter.

The final straw came in January 1984 when certain NAC executive
members in the eastern faction approved the purchase of thirty-six
vehicles, one for the business use of each NAC member. The NAC had
been promised vehicles for its work since 1977, but government back-
tracking on this commitment had built up impatience and anger

among NAC members. Learning of the ordered vehicles, Holding was infuriated at the NAC, seeing its action as direct defiance of his written policy on NAC vehicle procurement that he had sent to the NAC members the previous August (1983). What became known as 'the cars issue' cemented the NAC's image as a financially irresponsible organization. And it gave the DAA justification, if not reason, to take control of the NAC's financial administration. Consequently, Christmas 1983 marked the end of the 'review period' in the NAC's history of reform. 'The cars issue' together with the NAC's collapsing financial management system brought in the next stage of NAC reform, the 'receivership' stage.

The NAC's deterioration was characterized by internal political discord over the NAC chairman's resignation in early 1984, a resignation rumoured to have been influenced by the minister's office and by the financial management crisis. In March 1984, Holding literally placed the NAC under the financial receivership of the DAA, a condition described as 'the agency arrangement' (DAA 1985a: 23–4). The DAA was to retain financial authority until the NAC could demonstrate that it had regained control of its finances and had a proper accounting system in place. Holding also took a second, far more extraordinary step by calling on the auditor-general to examine the NAC's records. To control daily the NAC's expenditures, DAA officials were placed in the NAC's office, a step that predictably increased NAC resentment toward the bureaucracy and the minister. With a few new appointments in the NAC's secretariat, including the return of a former financial manager, the staff worked in a determined fashion to bring order to the NAC's financial management system. In the end, the report of the auditor-general (1984) was not the damning indictment of the NAC that some DAA officials had hoped for, even though it had shown need for improved financial management.

Relations between Holding and the NAC became further strained that same month when Coombs submitted his final report to Holding which recommended the abolition of the NAC (Coombs 1985). Coombs felt the stumbling block to self-reform was the NAC executive, and believed that it would actively damage efforts he proposed to develop a replacement body. His report was intended as a tool for Aboriginal discussion which was to eventuate in an Aboriginal created national political body. Coombs urged Holding to circulate his report widely and quickly among Aborigines so the replacement process could begin – the urgency for a reliable body being the need for Aborigines to participate in the development of a land rights policy. The senior DAA official reviewing Coombs's report for the minister intensely disliked it, on both ideological and practical grounds. This official did not support the idea of a strong national body, operating at arm's length from the government, and he found Coombs's proposed structure for a new body cumbersome. In addition, he had political reservations, citing its likely negative effect on the government in the anticipated federal election. He succeeded initially in withholding both the Coombs report and the auditor-general's report from the public. Both reports, although critical of the NAC, also reflected negatively on Holding's judgment in respect to the NAC. But the NAC felt the reports remained confidential so Holding could continue to control the NAC 'by holding them over our heads.' There was some truth in both strategies.

The DAA, despite its initial effort to support the NAC when Holding was first appointed, had opposed the ALP policy of reforming and strengthening the NAC. Most officials felt the reform policy was misguided, and as one said: 'There was a good deal of cynicism about the NAC. The department didn't want a national body, never had wanted one, felt it [the department] could do the job [of advising the minister].' Meantime, the land rights legislation had taken a turn for the worse in the eyes of many NAC members when Holding, before Christmas, had abruptly decided to set it aside temporarily in favour of developing heritage legislation to preserve Aboriginal sacred sites and objects. The NAC agreed to support this move, on the condition that Holding resume a strong land rights initiative after the federal election. Holding retained control of the NAC's financial administration when the NAC entered its final stage in June 1984.

With the election of Rob Riley to the NAC chairmanship in June, the pro-reform western faction came to power and started a process of 'renewal.' Riley tried to bring order to the NAC's political and administrative operations, his immediate goal being that of ending the DAA's 'agency arrangement' that controlled the NAC's financial management. The NAC's secretariat was reorganized, but it had yet to receive any of the new positions promised by Holding a year ago. Riley believed he had secured Holding's agreement to deliver the staff positions, having discussed the matter with Holding in a telephone conversation before deciding to run for the chairmanship. But misunderstanding prevailed and, when Riley took office, not only did the positions not materialize, the NAC's budget was cut back without any consultation with the NAC. In addition, after his election as chairman, Riley had personally written Holding a long and serious letter, urging cooperation between them, and seeking this support in ending the DAA's control of the NAC's financial operations. Holding received the letter and senior DAA officials made a pointed effort to determine if Riley himself had drafted it. But Holding never replied to Riley's letter. The relationship between Riley and Holding, never smooth at the best of times, deteriorated further by August as conflict over land rights policy sharpened. The NAC thought Holding should mount a solid public relations campaign to counteract the anti-land rights propaganda from the mining industry, but Holding had different views and was beginning to encounter problems internally over the policy.

Riley was an educated, articulate, leader who sought to make major changes in the NAC by developing a national perspective in its activities and outlook, by formulating NAC policies on several topics (e.g., NAC 1985a), and by addressing the need for organizational reform. To pursue reform, the NAC secretariat prepared a candid internal critique of the NAC's disjointed approach to reform (Ryan 1984), and Riley agreed to work jointly with the DAA to propose organizational reforms for the NAC. But in January 1985, when the NAC submitted its reform proposals for an expanded NAC to the DAA, Riley was shocked to experience rejection. The DAA officials, with few exceptions, had remained silent throughout the joint working sessions, and the NAC members interpreted this behaviour as agreement with the discussions. This rupture reinforced very sharp disagreement already mounting over the land rights policy, as Holding retreated from his initial position and the NAC demanded he hold the line (NAC 1985b; NAC *News* 1985).

Under Riley, the NAC became much more politically activist in its behaviour and critical of the government's stance on many issues, especially land rights policy and the alleged joint policy formulation process that Holding had promised on the matter. Committed to forging a new future for the NAC, Riley developed political alliances with the land councils in the powerful public campaign mounted in May 1985 to stop Holding's capitulation on land rights.

But before Riley had submitted the NAC proposal for its reform in January 1985, the DAA had *already* decided to abolish the NAC by terminating its funding, the only legal control a minister had over the NAC. This decision was finalized in the annual budget preparations by the DAA, and announced by Holding on 2 April 1985. The dying weeks of the NAC, in May and June 1985, were dramatic times as Aboriginal protests against Holding's land rights policy peaked.

Unseemly events transpired in the heat of the protests, including offers to restore the NAC, made by a senior Aboriginal bureaucrat to the Queensland faction, if the NAC would support the minister's land rights proposals. The official death of the NAC occurred on 30 June 1985.

Little public interest was evinced at the demise of the NAC, and a subsequent report (O'Donoghue 1986) commissioned by Holding on a successor body met with Aboriginal indifference. The succeeding minister of Aboriginal Affairs, Gerry Hand, renewed efforts to reform the policy structures in the Aboriginal Affairs portfolio (Hand 1987). In 1990 Hand established yet another government-designed, nationally elected Aboriginal body to advise the government on Aboriginal priorities, called the Aboriginal and Torres Strait Islander Commission (ATSIC; Hand 1987).

CONCLUSIONS

The purpose of this paper was to examine the relationship between self-determination, national pressure groups, and the nation-state by considering the case of attempted organizational reform of the Australian National Aboriginal Conference (NAC) in the mid-1980s. Nationalistic movements among Fourth World peoples invariably embodied the demands that they be permitted to establish their own political institutions through which they could shape their own policy preferences and deal with the nation-states. National pressure groups are clearly one type of political institution, more difficult to form because of their geographical and political distance from local people and organizations. But they are an essential component in the organizational repertoire of Fourth World peoples if national-level policies are to be coherently and forcefully influenced by them. And in keeping with self-determination as the broad political value informing these movements, it follows that Fourth World peoples will seek the freedom not only to establish these organizations but to reform them periodically – in effect to adapt them to changes in the political system so they are more effective policy instruments for both indigenous peoples and democratic nation-states. Indeed, democratic governments will have periodic if not continuous need for such national bodies, as they seek not only policy advice but more especially policy legitimacy.

In Australia, the history of national political organs for Aboriginal people has been one in which the nation-state has played an exceedingly strong interventionist role in comparison, for example, with Canada and Norway. This role took the form of creating and abolishing the NACC (1973–6) and then creating the NAC (1977) with such a disarticulated structure and a dearth of resources that it was predictably an ineffectual body for both Aboriginals and the government. When the ALP government came to power in 1983, significant political change was to occur. Under the guiding principle of self-determination in Aboriginal policy, this history of under-resourced and government-designed and imposed models of political organization was to end. And, under the minister's elaboration of this policy, Aboriginals were to reform and strengthen the NAC, converting it into a reliable, representative political organ. But the effort to reform the NAC turned into a decision to abolish it. This was definitely not a turn of fate that either the minister or the NAC envisaged at the outset.

Initially there were many factors in the NAC reform process that clearly encouraged organizational self-determination. These included an official government stance to strengthen the NAC as a major policy vehicle. They also included a policy value of self-determination for Aboriginals in general, and the NAC in particular, a strong ministerial commitment to reform at the outset, and ministerial provision of extraordinary resources (recognition, access, funding, personnel, and a policy function) to facilitate the reform. But paradoxically this policy of self-reform was imposed on an organization which, despite past demands for change, was unable to seize the opportunities it was provided and unable to avoid the problems these contained. In the early stages of reform, the minister's initiative affected the NAC differentially, reinforcing pre-existing power alignments which in part were based on different views of the organization's purpose and future. The minister's actions to encourage reform were well received by one faction, and his actions to provide resources were welcomed by both. But what was intended as a policy package to foster organizational self-determination, in fact fuelled organizational disarray and conflict. The provision of resources deflected attention from serious self-appraisal of the NAC's weaknesses; at the same time it enhanced the organization's weaknesses by overpowering its administrative capacity to manage the resources. It induced political strife by promising but never delivering personnel resources which the organization legitimately needed. The resources themselves became the focus of attention, and then through mismanagement, the rationale for escalating ministerial and bureaucratic control over the organization. Politically, the NAC was unable to develop a unified position on the need or direction of reform. The initial resistance to reform from the faction in power and the minister's desire to move to policy formation (e.g., land rights), provided a political rationale for the imposition of an external review of the organization. Despite the well-intended motives of Coombs, the review became, initially, a part of the problem, and then, later, a political mechanism for ministerial control of the organization. The NAC was in a state of political and administrative receivership to the minister and his bureaucracy when the NAC faction that supported reform eventually came to power. And when the new NAC leadership finally examined prospects for organizational change, the minister's goals had already shifted from containing the NAC to abolishing it. The NAC's refusal to legitimate the minister's major policy initiative (land rights) only strengthened the resolve to terminate the NAC's funding and thereby the organization.

In the short span of two years, the NAC had gone from rags to riches to receivership. Despite the efforts of the new NAC leadership to carry the NAC into a stage of rebirth and reform, the NAC was terminated by an act of ministerial retribution. The NAC had become a political liability to the minister and the department, whether it was in receivership or in activist reform. Furthermore, the policy environment originally intended to support the NAC reform (land rights) had failed to become the positive force initially envisaged by the minister and the NAC. The policy environment had been dominated by a single policy (land rights) which initially selectively affected Aborigines, and later, because of substantive changes to it at the cabinet level, diminished significantly the few benefits it might have bestowed on Aborigines. Consequently, the NAC could not use land rights policy as an issue on which to develop organizational solidarity, nor could the NAC provide policy legitimation on land rights, as the minister sought.

The idea of containing rather than abolishing the NAC had been considered by the bureaucracy, on the grounds that if the government terminated the NAC it would only, in time, replace it, given the eventual need or desire for Aboriginal advice and policy legitimation. This has transpired in the creation of another national body, ATSIC, the Aboriginal and Torres Strait Islander Commission.

Australia has institutionalized the practice of government intervention and control of national political organizations for Aboriginals. Organizational self-determination for Fourth World peoples in Australia remains an idea that has yet to be realized. Ultimately, self-determination for Aboriginal organizations is in the best interests of the nation-state, for bodies that lack Aboriginal legitimacy also lack the ability to legitimate government policies, a process required in democratic political systems.

Acknowledgments

Research for this paper was funded solely by the Social Sciences and Humanities Research Council of Canada. Although interviews were conducted in 1983, 1984, and 1985 on the NAC in Canberra and Darwin, Australia, the bulk of the work was carried out in Canberra and other major cities from September to December 1986. I am genuinely grateful to former members of the NAC, to government officials (in the Department of Aboriginal Affairs, the Department of the Prime Minister, the Department of Finance, and the Public Service Board), to Clyde Holding, Nugget Coombs, Lois O'Donoghue, and many others for their helpful interviews. Thanks are also due to the Australian Institute for Aboriginal Studies and the DAA for granting me access to the archival files on the NAC. All errors in this paper are mine.

NOTES

1 This definition derives from the United Nations 1960 Declaration on the Granting of Independence to Colonial Countries and Peoples, cited in Davies (1991: 776).
2 In Canada, First Nation Indians reorganized the National Indian Brotherhood into the Assembly of First Nations beginning in 1980, and in Norway, the national government passed the Sami Act 1984 which brought into being a nationally elected body of thirty-one Sami in 1989 called the Samiting (Sami Parliament).
3 'Aboriginal Group Calls for Embargoes at UN Forum,' *The Age*, 29 April 1981; 'Investigation Sought: Aboriginal Body Beyond Term,' *Canberra Times*, 20 February 1981.
4 *NAC Newsletter*, 1982, 'Minister Asked to Censure ADC,' September 1982, p. 21; 'Aboriginal Groups Trade Blow,' *NT News*, 16 June 1982.
5 NAC Minutes of the NAC Executive Meeting, Sydney–Canberra, 14–17 March 1983, Appendix D, Transcript of Meeting with Clyde Holding, p. 24.
6 NAC briefing document 'For Discussion Wednesday, 16th March, 1983,'

by Research Director, NAC Secretariat. Also, NAC document 'Position Paper: The Future of the N.A.C. under an A.L.P. Federal Government,' 17 March 1983, by the Research Director, NAC.

7 NAC document 'Role and Structure of the NAC: First Report, NAC Research Unit, July 1983.'

8 Interviews with Dr H.C. Coombs, Australian National University, Canberra, 22 September and 2 October 1986.

9 NAC *Media Release*, Perth, 4 November 1983, as reported in the *Canberra Times*, 7 November 1983: Transcript, Radio Program 'AM' on ABC, 7 November 1983. Quotations are from NAC document 'Statement to NAC Executive by Rob Riley, Canberra, 3/11/83,' in the NAC transcript of the NAC Executive Meeting 31 October to 3 November 1983, Appendix.

REFERENCES

Aboriginal Newsletter. 1983a. 'Minister Visits NT.' March, p. 1
– 1983b. 'Minister Forecasts Historic Period for Aboriginals.' July, pp. 1 and 4
Assembly of First Nations (AFN). 1986. *Our Land, Our Government, Our Future, Our Heritage.* Ottawa: Assembly of First Nations
Auditor-General. 1984. *Report on Inspection and Audit of National Aboriginal Conference,* 24 September. Canberra: Office of the Auditor-General
Australian Labor Party (ALP). 1982. *Australian Labor Party: 1982 Platform Constitution and Rules.* Canberra: ALP National Secretariat
– 1983. *Aboriginal Affairs Policy 1983: Labor's Programme for Self-determination.* Senator Susan Ryan, Federal Opposition Spokesperson on Aboriginal Affairs. February Canberra: Australian Labor Party
Beckett, Jeremy (ed.). 1988. *Past and Present: The Construction of Aboriginality.* Canberra: Aboriginal Studies Press
Cardinal, Harold. 1977. *The Rebirth of Canada's Indians.* Edmonton: Hurtig
Connor, Walker. 1973. 'The Politics of Ethnonationalism.' *Journal of International Affairs* 27(1): 1–21
Coombs, H.C. 1983. *Provisional Draft – A National Aboriginal Political Organisation.* 16 December. [Unpublished document]. Canberra: Australian National University
– 1985. *The Role of the National Aboriginal Conference* [April 1984]. Canberra: Australian Government Publishing Service
Department of Aboriginal Affairs (DAA). 1985a. *Documents Relating to the National Aboriginal Conference (NAC).* Canberra: Department of Aboriginal Affairs

– 1985b. *Report of the Task Force on the Restructuring of the* NAC, March. Canberra: Department of Aboriginal Affairs

Dene Nation. 1977. 'A Proposal to the Government and People of Canada,' in M. Watkins (ed.), *Dene Nation – The Colony Within.* Toronto: University of Toronto Press, pp. 182–7

Davies, Maureen. 1991. 'Aboriginal Rights in International Law: Human Rights,' in Bradford Morse (ed.), *Aboriginal Peoples and the Law.* Ottawa: Carleton University Press, pp. 745–94

Elliott, Jean. 1984. 'Emerging Ethnic Nationalism in the Canadian Northwest Territories.' *Canadian Review of Studies in Nationalism* 11(2): 231–44

Erasmus, Georges. 1977. 'We the Dene,' in M. Watkins (ed.), *Dene Nation – The Colony Within.* Toronto: University of Toronto Press, pp. 177–81

Hand, Gerry. 1987. *Foundations for the Future: Policy Statement.* Speech to the House of Representatives, 10 December. Canberra: Australian Government Publishing Service

Hiatt, Les. 1976. *The Role of the National Aboriginal Consultative Committee,* 4 November. Canberra: Australian Government Publishing Service

Kienetz, A. 1986. 'Decolonization in the North: Canada and the United States.' *Canadian Review of Studies in Nationalism* 13(1): 57–77

– 1987. 'Ethnonationalism and Decolonization in Greenland and Northern Eurasia.' *Canadian Review of Studies in Nationalism* 14(2): 247–59

– 1988. 'Metis Nationalism and the Concept of a Metis Land Base in Canada's Prairie Provinces.' *Canadian Review of Studies in Nationalism* 15(1–2): 11–18

Long, Anthony J., and Menno Boldt. 1988. 'Self-determination and Extra-legal Action: The Foundations of Native Indian Protests.' *Canadian Review of Studies in Nationalism* 15(1–2): 111–19

National Aboriginal Conference (NAC). 1985a. *Directions: Policies of the National Aboriginal Conference.* 3 May. Canberra: NAC

– 1985b. *National Aboriginal Conference Response to federal government's Preferred Position on National Land Rights Legislation.* 21 February. NAC *Media Release.* Canberra: NAC

NAC *News.* 1984. 'Chairman Reviews NAC Developments at Open Day [of the Adelaide Aboriginal College), 1 December],' February: 10–11

– 1985. 'NAC Rejects Federal Govt [sic] Land Rights Model,' 1(4): 1

O'Donoghue, Lois. 1986. *An Aboriginal and Islander Consultative Organisation.* (September) Canberra: DAA

Pross, A. Paul. 1986. *Group Politics and Public Policy.* Toronto: Oxford University Press

Randell, Alan, and Reg Shelley. 1983. *Management Action Workshop Number*

Two, Queensland State Branch of the National Aboriginal Conference, Held at Cairns, August 1983. Rockhampton, Queensland: Capricornia Institute of Advanced Education

Riggs, Fred W. 1986. 'What Is Ethnic? What Is National? Let's Turn the Tables.' *Canadian Review of Studies in Nationalism* 13(1): 111–23

Ryan, Hiram. 1984. *Role and Structure of the NAC.* Canberra: NAC

Sawchuk, Joe. 1978. *The Metis of Manitoba.* Toronto: Peter Martin

Viner, Ian. 1977. Ministerial Statement on National Aboriginal Conference [NAC Charter]. House of Representatives. *Debates,* 30 May, pp. 2104–11

Weaver, Sally M. 1983. 'Australian Aboriginal Policy: Aboriginal Pressure Groups or Advisory Bodies?' Parts I and II. *Oceania* 54: 1–22; 54: 85–108

White, Philip L. 1985. 'What Is Nationality?' *Canadian Review of Studies in Nationalism* 12(1): 1–23

Wolf, Ken. 1986. 'Ethnic Nationalism: An Analysis and a Defense.' *Canadian Review of Studies in Nationalism* 13(1): 99–109

CHAPTER 4

History and Culture in the Generation of Ethnic Nationalism

Adrian Tanner

In 1989–90 a British television series was in production that dealt with indigenous peoples in different parts of the world, but, unlike previous television collections of ethnographic documentaries, the point of the series was not to draw attention to indigenous peoples who are disappearing, but to those who are actively resisting threats to their autonomy. The single Canadian example in the series was the Innu (Montagnais–Naskapi Indians)[1] and their campaign of opposition to low-level military flight training, which is being conducted by several European NATO states over their unceded land in Labrador and adjacent Quebec. This case seems to exemplify small pre-industrial peoples holding out for their way of life against the power of the industrial state.[2]

The British series producer chose the Innu case in consultation with Survival International of London (Brody and Markham 1990), and in so doing had to turn down several other possibilities, including a film on the violent struggle of the Melanesian highland people on the Iryan Jaya – Papua New Guinea border, who were fighting the Indonesian government. While the producer's choice may indicate more about the tastes of European television audiences than about which of these cases best exemplifies indigenous resistance, the Innu, nevertheless, are a striking example of indigenous nationalism turned against the modern state. This is because the Innu protest raises fundamental questions about the legitimacy of settler states' treatment of the indigenous peoples and of their lands.

The case is striking as well because of the David and Goliath proportions of the confrontation (albeit a non-violent one). A few Innu succeeded, for a period at least, in defying the combined forces of the federal, provincial, and municipal governments, and those of several NATO governments, as well as a large and well-funded Labrador pro-development lobby. This ragtag collection of men, women, and children using Ghandian tactics occupied test-bombing ranges and climbed airbase perimeter fences to lie on runways, stopping million-dollar high-technology war machines from taking off (Wadden 1991). But more remarkable, I believe, is the radical indigenous nationalist ideology that stimulated the political actions of the Innu demonstrators, an ideology that had already inspired a variety of earlier confrontations between the Innu and the state on a variety of issues.

The Innu are certainly not the only indigenous people to have adopted a strong ethnonationalist political ideology, or to engage in political actions of radical opposition to the state. However, most other contemporary Canadian cases that come to mind, such as the Lubicon, the Temiagami Nishnabwe, the Gitksan–Wet'suuet'an, the Dene, and the James Bay Cree, are groups that implicitly accept the institutions of the state, and are, in different ways, simply seeking to negotiate for themselves a more satisfactory position within that state framework or, at most, seeking only a modest alteration of those institutional arrangements. The Innu have followed the indigenous ethnonationalist idea further toward one of its logical conclusions, directly challenging the fundamental legitimacy of the state, denying the authority that provincial and federal laws and courts assert over them and their lands. To do this they have frequently turned to international arenas as the context for political action.

From the colonial beginnings, Canadian aboriginal peoples have expressed their political complaints against the emerging state, but only relatively infrequently, from the Red River Rebellion to the 1990 Oka crisis, have they done so by actions openly challenging the authority of the state. The undermining of community leadership through government institutions of indirect rule, the discouragement of political contacts between aboriginal groups, and the use of political encapsulation and brokerage, along with widespread internal social breakdown of the aboriginal communities, all combined to diffuse most concerted opposition (Tanner 1983a).

Until the late 1970s the Innu, like many other northern Canadian aboriginal hunters, seemed to have been overwhelmed by the impact of development, and unable to put up any effective resistance to this process. For example, as late as 1969 as vast area of some of their prime hunting lands, together with their hunting equipment which had, as it normally was, been left in their bush camps, was flooded by the Churchill Falls hydroelectric project. The Innu offered no resistance, organized no public protest. And yet by the late 1970s a movement centred among the Innu of Sheshatshit, Labrador, were espousing an ideology of pan-Innu ethnic nationalism aimed directly at the legitimacy of the Canadian state, an ideology which would subsequently determine how they would react when their territory began to be used for intensive, high-speed, low-level jet training in the early 1980s. How do we account for this change?

The political scientist Walker Connor believes that ethnic national-ism only comes out of the self-awareness of the group in question. Moreover, he traces the origins of ethnic nationalist movements to what he sees as a specific historical event, the emergence of the *idea* of self-determination among self-conscious ethnic groups, something that he says occurred for the first time in the late nineteenth century within the nation-state context (Connor 1973). While the Innu them-selves claim that their own nationalism originates in their prehistoric identity as a people, in what follows I will illustrate what I see as the social origins of this core ethnic nationalist idea, and its significance as a counter-claim to the practices of state nationalism.

Connor's observation raises many questions, however. He appar-ently considers ethnic nationalism a different phenomenon from the kind of nationalism by which indigenous peoples, including those in North America like the Innu, were initially dealt with centuries ago by the newly arrived Europeans, that is, on what was in some sense a nation-to-nation basis. Not only were the aboriginal groups ap-proached by the Europeans as autonomous collectivities, but they responded as such, making alliances, trading agreements, and peace treaties. Only later was their autonomy reduced to a level where political relations with the state placed them in the position of subor-dinate dependants, often obliging them to communicate with the state through self-appointed middlemen, such as missionaries. Yet we know little about whether or not the proto-historic Innu had a con-cept equivalent to national self-determination, since the only evidence we have of this issue is from the viewpoint of what increasingly became the more powerful European side of the relationship.

Whatever was the situation at first contact, the recent (re)assertion of Canadian indigenous peoples' nationalism and calls for autonomy does indeed, as Connor suggests, seem to have followed from the development of their self-conscious identity as a people. In the case of the aboriginal people of Labrador and to some degree among those in adjacent Quebec, this new identity has been marked, for example, by their insistence (starting around 1978) on being called 'Innu,' instead of the previous labels applied to them of 'Montagnais' or 'Naskapi.' It also coincides with having their territory referred to as 'Nitassinan.'

Connor's observation also leaves open the question of why ethno-nationalist ideas are taken up by some particular ethnic groups, but not others. Also, into what forms of action, political or otherwise, do such ideas of ethnic self-determination become translated and expressed? I am concerned in particular with why the Innu of Labrador have adopted the particular version of the ethnonationalist ideology that they have, and have taken the kinds of political actions they have following the adoption of this ideology. While it may seem that the ideology and the actions flowing from it appeared suddenly, I will argue that this form of ethnic politics has its roots in estab-lished Innu cultural values and in the Innu historical experience. The form of Innu ethnic politics contrasts sharply with that of the other aboriginal group in Labrador, the Inuit. I therefore believe that Connor's ideas need to be modified with a sensitivity to the approach summed up in Parkin's phrase 'the cultural definition of political re-sponse' (1978).

SOURCES OF IDEOLOGY

When aboriginal people oppose the use of their lands by others the suggestion is sometimes made, usually by their adversaries, that they have been influenced by outside agitators (Armitage and Kennedy 1989). Comparatively little has been published analysing the influence or lack of it that outsiders have on the development of political ideas (but see La Rusic et al. 1979 and Beyer Broch 1983). Innu adopted ethnonationalism at around the same time they were having increas-ing contacts with sympathetic outsiders, and these people should not be overlooked as possible sources of new ideas and ideologies. Before 1970 the Innu had been relatively isolated from the mainstream of the Canadian indigenous political movement, after which a number of non-Innu visitors, allies, supporters, employees, and professional consultants, non-indigenous as well as from other indigenous groups, came to live and work with them. Innu leaders themselves have also travelled widely in Canada and in Europe. However, such external sources of ideas do not, in this particular case, adequately account for Innu nationalism.

The tendency was for Innu leaders to focus on an analysis of their own situation, one which they knew far better than any outsider, and in so doing they did not make reference to, or seem to take their inspiration from, the similarity of their situation with that of other groups. However, one particular early non-Innu employee in their political organization, the Naskapi Montagnais Innu Association (NMIA), now renamed the Innu Nation (IN), was influential, introducing the terminology of the decolonization movement. In addition, a number of university-based social scientists who conducted research on the Innu were generally critical of government programs and policies, making use of some version of dependency theory (Armitage 1991: ch. 6; Charest 1983; Savard 1979; Tanner 1983b; Tanner and Armitage 1986). There have also been a number of young priests who supported various Innu political campaigns and who were probably influenced by the doctrine of liberation theology. Still other supporters from religiously based and volunteer groups like Aboriginal Rights Coalition (Project North) and the Mennonite Central Committee have viewed the situation of the Innu in light of the general critique of hinterland and Third World development processes. In their travels, the Innu have also encountered many different political leaders of other indigenous groups, in Canada and abroad. Yet while the Innu were exposed to several foreign ideologies and analyses applied by others to their situation, these influences do not account for why they adopted their own particular ethnonationalist ideology.

It could also be argued that the federal government is another potential external source of ethnonationalist ideas. The aboriginal peoples of Newfoundland did not come under federal jurisdiction when the provinces entered Confederation in 1949, but, from their knowledge of the situation of their relatives based in Quebec, who do come under federal administration, the Labrador Innu know the implication of the demand that they be officially recognized as 'registered' Indians, thus making them eligible for access to special federal programs. 'Indian status' can be seen as a federal government-sponsored legal form of ethnic separation, possibly even implying a mild form of ethnic nationalism. However, the Labrador Innu have not chosen to pursue 'Indian status,' either as a means of expressing their ethnic identity or as a strategy to achieve the political reunification of the Innu people as a whole. In my view it is significant for the understanding of Innu political ideas to appreciate why they have, up to now, been reluctant to exercise this particular avenue to express their ethnic solidarity.[3]

Labrador Innu leaders choose their own political path based largely on internal considerations. For instance, in 1975 and 1976 I was employed by the Labrador Innu to conduct land claims research, at around the same time as I was also working on the negotiation of the James Bay and Northeastern Quebec Agreement on behalf of the Naskapi band of Schefferville. I could have been described at the time as a proponent of the (albeit limited) 'self-determination' opportunities offered by Indian Act registration and a land claims settlement. The Innu have debated the options of both registration and land claims among themselves, both at the time and since. An objective assessment would have to conclude that my actual influence on Innu political ideology, not to mention practice, as judged by the actions of the Labrador Innu on these two issues, was minimal or non-existent. Neither registration nor land claims have been seriously pursued, and the Labrador Innu act with a strong mistrust of existing government programs, federal and provincial.

It is thus important to distinguish between the ideas introduced by advisers and those of the Innu themselves, even though the task is sometimes made difficult when speeches and letters were attributed to leaders, especially in the early years of their formal organization, but were actually drafted by non-Innu advisers. Nevertheless, it was the Innu leadership who made the choices regarding the adoption of political ideas, goals, and strategies, and these ideas then became reflected in the policies of the leadership. For example, in 1983 the election for the president of NMIA was between two candidates: a former president, a particularly articulate leader, who counselled cooperation with the military as the best way for the Innu to turn the problem of low-level flights to advantage, and his younger opponent, who advocated uncompromising opposition. The majority of the people of the larger Innu community of Sheshatshit clearly favoured the latter opinion, and the second candidate won the election easily. The candidate who had favoured cooperation then changed his position entirely to become a major spokesperson for the confrontational strategy, and since then there has been solid community consensus on this issue.

INNU POLITICAL ACTIVITIES, 1973–90

Besides the growing anti-military campaign, the Labrador Innu have been engaged in various other political issues over the past two decades. A pattern emerged from these issues which was characterized by both the confrontational style of Innu ethnopolitics and the gradual adoption of a specific ethnonationalist ideology.

Political Autonomy

The first formal political organization of the Labrador Innu took place in the late 1960s. After a period of token 'chiefs' who had been selected by European authorities, primarily the missionaries, political leaders who began to represent the real interests of the Innu to non-Innu society emerged. In 1973, the year that federal money first became available to fund aboriginal organizations, these leaders began to gain some influence. The government's intention with this funding was that it would only support one 'status' Indian organization and one 'non-status' or metis one for each province, so the Innu of Quebec joined in the Indians of Quebec Association (IQA) – which also included Mohawk, East Cree, Attikameg, and Micmac members – and those in Labrador joined in the Native Association of Newfoundland and Labrador (NANL) along with the Micmacs of the island part of Newfoundland. From 1973 to 1977 Innu politics were dominated by the previously mentioned particularly articulate leader, who was aggressive in his public complaints against the injustices suffered by his people. He employed these complaints in a diverse and a pragmatic manner, rather than pursuing any particular ideological objective or following a program of indigenous nationalism.

In 1976 the leadership of the Innu of Sheshatshit spearheaded a break from NANL by the Labrador Innu, to form the Naskapi Montagnais Innu Association (NMIA). The rationale for this move was the ethnic distinctiveness of the Innu, and the consequent problems they had in working within an organization dominated by the Micmacs. Their aim with the new organization was to gain a greater proportion of the limited available funds for the Innu, on the argument that the Innu were more in need, and more legitimately aboriginal than were the Micmacs, who they portrayed as having substantially lost their aboriginal culture.

Aggressive actions such as this, which have tended to engender hostile political relations between the Innu and other groups, are not uncommon. In pursuing their own specific political goals, Labrador Innu leaders will often deal in an openly assertive manner with any others who express aims different from their own. This is even the case when dealing with leaders of the larger neighbouring aboriginal groups, the Labrador Inuit or the Quebec Innu, and it is also often the case when dealing with non-aboriginals. Even allies, if they do not agree with a leader's aims and strategies, may find themselves dealt with in an unexpectedly hostile manner.

One possible explanation for this endemic pattern of aggressiveness is to relate it to the lack of an Innu tradition of having specific authority figures. Another is the particularly strong sense an Innu person has of his or her own personal autonomy. Thus, a particular Innu leader always speaks his own mind, but, depending on the context, may or may not be considered to be speaking on behalf of his whole group. This assertiveness works surprisingly well within a largely equalitarian group like the Innu. When agreement is expressed, it is to be trusted. The Innu often hold a unified position that is arrived at by means of this form of group consensus, but in periods of uncertainly and change there may be several positions held by various leaders or spokespersons. This sometimes makes it difficult to avoid misunderstandings and maintain smooth political relations with outsiders.

Land Claims

Research in support of a Labrador Innu Land Claim was begun in 1974, mainly because government funding for this purpose was available, and because the Micmac on the island of Newfoundland, who at the time were part of NANL, the same association as the Innu belonged to, were strongly interested in the pursuit of a land claim. As explained above, by the time the research was complete in 1977 the Labrador Innu had broken off to form their own independent organization, NMIA, and they made use of the influential adviser referred to above to formulate their claim. Much of their statement of claim was either based on or influenced by the Dene Declaration (reprinted in Ponting and Gibbins 1980: 351–2), including the demand that the aboriginal group be given extensive control over the entire territory of the claim. In fierce anti-colonial rhetoric, they presented themselves and their land as sovereign, and chastised Canada at length as a colonial trespasser (part of the claim document is reproduced in Tanner and Henderson 1992: 160–3). The idea of the Newfoundland government playing any part in negotiations was rejected. They were unwilling to draw sharp boundaries around their claim area, in part because they saw this as representing a European real-estate view of land, and probably also because they wished to hold open the opportunity of a combined claim with the Quebec Innu.[4]

Although the federal Department of Indian Affairs accepted the legal validity of the Innu claim, they also sharply criticised its radical tone and its demands. They made it clear that early negotiations were unlikely. Subsequently, the claims of both the Labrador Inuit and the Quebec Innu (the claims bordering on either side of that of the Labrador Innu) were placed on a short list for negotiation, but that of the Labrador Innu was not. However, this did not concern the Innu since, following from their increasingly nationalist position and their disputing the legitimacy of Canadian sovereignty over their lands, Innu leaders were less and less willing to negotiate within the framework laid down by Indian Affairs, in consultation with the province of Newfoundland.

Recently, as Innu opposition to low-level flying has started to show success, opponents of the Innu campaign began to claim that its real aim was not really an objection to low-level flying, but a strategy to strengthen their bargaining power in future land claims negotiations. This idea is totally erroneous, although it is one of great interest in revealing non-Innu cultural ideas, because of the way it misunderstands Innu political motives, assuming there must be a hidden rationale of self-interest, and failing to accept at face value the significance of Innu ethnic nationalist assertions. This mistaken notion was apparently taken seriously enough by Indian Affairs officials that in 1989 an offer was made that, if the Innu would allow low-level flying to continue without opposition, the government was willing to begin land claims talks. Thus, success in one political arena appears to have brought a form of empowerment in another, but one which the Innu had little or no use for. Even an uncalled-for form of empowerment may influence a relatively powerless group. While it remains to be seen if this offer will move the Innu in the direction of trying to find an acceptable accommodation with the government's conception of land claims, Innu leaders have made tentative steps to soften their opposition to these claims, in that a lawyer has been hired and told to try to speed up negotiations. Talks toward a framework agreement are under way.

Game Laws

Next to the issue of military training, the most significant public protests organized by the Labrador Innu have concerned game laws. In Labrador, government game laws for the general public only effectively began to replace informal community regulations in the

1950s, and government hunting regulations are strongly influenced by local non-Innu political pressure (Bergerud 1967). Licences for caribou hunting are now required for Natives and non-Natives alike, and in the southern half of Labrador the Innu had to obtain them by lottery, along with all other residents. Increasingly, Innu hunters in the bush began to be arrested for various violations.

Starting in 1976, the NMIA began to fight such charges in court, on the basis of an aboriginal rights argument. However, legal representation was not used in all such cases, and when they were lost, as they usually were, they were not appealed. These trials were far more important as occasions for the expression of Innu nationalist sentiments than they were attempts to win acquittal according to European rules. The Innu national flag was first displayed publicly during one of these trials, and these trials became important public events to which the whole community of Sheshatshit (including the children, who were taken out of school on trial days) turned out. The only such cases that Innu defendants won were on technicalities.

In 1977 a case of caribou hunting in violation of provincial game laws made the headlines, and the Innu accused received considerable sympathy of non-Innu in Labrador and elsewhere, since the public perception was that the accused were clearly in need of food and were doing no more than pursuing their traditional activities. The minister concerned was finally forced to agree to negotiate the issue. However, at these talks the inexperienced Innu leadership agreed to settle on the basis of merely oral understandings, which the government failed to live up to, as soon as the publicity had died down.

By way of contrast, a case ten years later that began in a similar manner had quite different results, demonstrating how the situation of Innu ethnopolitics and local reaction to them had changed in the interim. In the spring of 1988 the Innu learned that after a closure of several years the government was about to allow a limited hunt of the Mealy Mountain herd near Goose Bay. Rather than trust to receiving no more than a small proportion of licences by lottery, the Innu leadership decided to take matters into their own hands and conduct a limited pre-emptive harvest for themselves, an activity which they did not try to hide from the authorities. Unlike the incident in 1977, the reaction was not public support for Innu subsistence hunting rights, but a public outcry against them. This opposition occurred because in the interim, due to their successful campaign against military training in the area, the Innu had made themselves despised by their neighbours in Happy Valley and Goose Bay, many of whom depended on the military for their jobs.

Innu Political Unity

Given that the focus of my paper is on the Labrador Innu, the section of Innu society which has developed a particularly radical ethnonationalist position, I will not deal in detail with the Quebec-based Innu or with their political organization, the Conseil des Attikameg et des Montagnais (CAM), formed after the IQA broke up. Even though CAM and NMIA–IN (that is, the Naskapi Montagnais Innu Association and its successor, the Innu Nation) are often on the same side of an issue (such as in their opposition to military activities), their approach is usually quite different, and each frequently ends up working at cross-purposes to the other. As an example of the difference in political approaches, some Quebec Innu leaders campaigned on behalf of Prime Minister Mulroney, whose riding includes some Quebec Innu communities, and have joined the native caucus of the Conservative Party, something that would be unimaginable under present circumstances for Labrador Innu.

Since the late 1970s one of the aims of NMIA–IN has been to bring about the political unification of the Innu living on both sides of the Quebec–Labrador border, an aim which has prompted the intense suspicion of CAM. In 1982 this aim resulted in the formation of the Innu National Council – *Innu Kanantuapatshet* – (INC) at a meeting to which elders from all the Innu communities were invited. Around the same time the Innu, along with Micmacs, Lakota, and Southern Cheyenne, formed an organization called the Four Directions Council (FDC). This organization, the brainchild of an American aboriginal rights lawyer, had non-government organization (NGO) consultative status with the United Nations, and the Labrador Innu used it to present their argument that they were a distinct national people. Since neither the INC nor the FDC had government funding, to the extent that they were entities expressing pan-Innu concerns they were effectively the creations of NMIA. Some further meetings were held, and they continued to issue press releases for some time, but ceased to be active after about 1985.

Not only does CAM feel that NMIA–IN's radical positions are counter-productive, but the individuals in the Quebec Innu communities who respond to NMIA–IN's approaches tend to do so because they happen to be dissatisfied with the leadership of CAM at the particular time. Since these factional politics within CAM are ever-changing, this means that the allies of NMIA within the Quebec Innu communities are fairly unstable. However, one Quebec leader has been a consistent supporter of the NMIA–IN concept of Innu unity, although he has had little influence in CAM. The result is that, apart from expressions made in the context of large pan-Innu religious gatherings, and in Innu popular music, the assertion and mobilization of pan-Innu ethnic unity has as yet had little tangible success.

Both the political organization and the political ideology of the two provincially based groups are quite different, despite their common culture. As will be seen later on in this paper, part of my argument as to why the Labrador Innu have adopted the political position they have rests on conditions that are peculiar and distinctive to the Labrador group. These conditions therefore also account to some degree for why the Quebec Innu have not adopted the same ideology.

The Ideology of Political Independence

While documents using anti-colonial and Innu nationalist ideas were written during the early period of NMIA, it was not until the 1977 land claim that Innu leaders began publicly supporting actions and making speeches along these Innu nationalist lines, using the language of decolonization and self-determination. The assertion of their claim to political independence from Canada was outlined in private meetings with supporters in 1981 and after that more publicly. The public use of this Innu nationalist ideology apparently predates these events, but occurred outside Canada, in speeches to UN bodies in Geneva, which the Innu attended first in the late 1970s. With their membership in the short-lived Four Directions Council, these appearances in Geneva were more frequent. At first these presentations were made in the context of such things as opposition to the patriation of the Canadian constitution from Britain, petitions for the decolonization of the Innu, and opposition to mining and other development on their land. Starting in 1983, these presentations included opposition to the military use of low-level flight training over the Innu homeland. However, public statements made in Labrador during this period were not very explicit or detailed regarding particular ethnic nationalist aspects of the policy.

Instead, the claim of political autonomy is to be found more in the specific actions taken. The nationalist ideology has more recently been expressed within Labrador, for example, as part of statements made during court appearances, such as when charges are laid following a demonstration against low-level flying. One particular Innu leader, who usually has a position in the second rank of the leadership, has developed the facility for speeches asserting Innu nationalism and Innu independence.

Opposition to Development Projects

The Innu have made several formal presentations to hearings, opposing such projects as a uraniam mine in Labrador, further hydroelectric projects, and a proposed aluminum smelter. While they have questioned the environmental and social effects of such projects, their main arguments have been that the projects violate Innu territorial rights.

Commissioned Research

The Innu have pursued their ethnonationalist ideas through the commissioning of research projects. Like other northern aboriginal peoples, they have a strong ideological focus on the maintenance of hunting, given the impact of urbanization and increasing state control of wildlife. This interest is seen in the concern with programs in support of the hunting and trapping economy (Andrews 1984; see also Government of Newfoundland 1984). Innu leaders have also commissioned research on a project with nationalistic implications, involving the estimation of the value of the economic rents owed to them for resources like iron ore, hydroelectric power, and wood taken from Innu lands (Grant 1981).

Opposition to Military Training

While the Innu have campaigned from 1981 onwards against low-level flying, they first did so in a way that fitted in with their general strategy of focusing their message outside Canada by using their existing contacts in Europe. This campaign grew to become the major focus of their political actions, as they began occupations of bombing ranges and runways in 1987. Up to this point the Innu had directed little of their political action toward the Canadian public. This neglect of a domestic focus for their political activities was in part determined by their position regarding the illegitimacy of the Canadian state's claims to authority over them and their lands. However, the result of the occupations of the runways and the practice bombing range was an increase in the interest shown by the Canadian press. The Innu became drawn by new supporters into a major campaign within Canada, and, from the Innu perspective, the unexpected mobilizing of further supporters of the Innu cause throughout Canada. In large part this new support came from the peace movement's participation in the campaign to stop low-level flying.

The move to political actions directed towards a domestic as well as an international audience also coincided with the emergence of a new group of Innu leaders, for the first time including several women, and these people were more pragmatic in their aims and more open to new strategies. However, the tendency of the Innu to reject the authorized state mechanisms of conflict resolution did not change. The Innu persist in refusing to recognize the authority of the courts when charged. However, the Innu began to use the courts in a more strategic manner, for example with an attempt to obtain an injunction halting low-level flying on the grounds that no environmental impact assessment had been completed. They also maintained their policy of not cooperating with the military authorities, for example, refusing to identify their campsites, saying that it is not their obligation to tell authorities where they are going in their own land, and adding that when they had given authorities their camp locations in the past they were still overflown. They have refused to participate in the environmental assessment of low-level flying and the proposed NATO base, although they did gain intervenor status, and have conducted a thorough critique of the Department of National Defence's environmental impact statement.

To conclude this summary of Labrador Innu ethnopolitical activities over the past twenty years, they can be seen as having gone through three stages. Up to 1977 the organization was dominated by the previously mentioned leader who was a pragmatic power broker and an adviser who advocated international action and an anticolonial approach. From 1977 to 1986 a pan-Innu ethnic-nationalist ideology was taken up by Innu leaders and an international strategy was employed which focused on challenging the actions of the Canadian government before various UN agencies. Following this, a new group of leaders emerged, whose agenda became focused on the specific issue of the use of Innu land for military low-level flight training, using protest actions which were increasingly directed at Canadian public opinion, and assisted by non-Innu domestic allies.

THE RAPID LOSS OF INNU AUTONOMY

I now return to the question I posed earlier of why the Labrador Innu adopted the relatively radical ethnonationalist ideology they did. Three considerations as to why such ideas were taken up and acted upon will be raised here.

The first has to do with the degree to which the idea of ethnic nationalism found a compatible setting within the pre-existing cultural ideas and institutions of the group. I do not have space here to further elaborate the point, but I would argue that radical ethnonationalism found a compatible home among the Innu in part because it was consistent with the stress already found in Innu culture on social equality, and their open access to territory and resources, one well suited to such a nomadic people. Also, their concept of *Innu*, or 'person,' allows them to portray themselves in contradistinction to other neighbouring groups, both indigenous and non-indigenous. Moreover, competition is endemic among the Innu leadership, as it was within the historic nomadic residential hunting group, where a common method of handling disputes was through physical separation of the disputants into a new arrangement of residential units. Thus, problems with their neighbours quite naturally lead to strategies of withdrawal and the re-establishment of local self-determination.

The second factor in considering the relevance of culture to the adoption of political ideology is the degree and manner in which the ethnic group in question finds its autonomy being limited by the dominant culture. On this question the Innu are little different from all other Canadian indigenous groups in having lost a significant part of their real autonomy since European contact, due to the activities of their non-aboriginal neighbours, from the unilateral construction of development projects by corporations and governments to the imposition of state legal and administrative systems. What is distinctive about the Innu experience of this process, and in particular that of the Innu of Labrador, is the rapidity with which they became exposed to these kinds of restrictions to their autonomy.

Until the 1950s the Innu had virtually sole occupation of the interior of Labrador. The fur trade first entered the region only indirectly, first from posts along the St Lawrence, starting in the seventeenth century. Direct trade within Labrador only began in the nineteenth century. Several interior posts were opened, but they were closed again after only a few years. Monopoly conditions, which were normal within much of the fur trade elsewhere, were never successfully established among the Innu. The fur trade had some especially devastating impacts on the more northern Innu, because of its incompatibility with caribou hunting, which remained the mainstay of their subsistance. But the result of the fur trade was not the subservience of the Innu to the demands of regular trade, as occurred in other northern regions, but rather their relative marginalization from it, as their role as trappers for the trade was largely taken over by others and as game supplies declined.

The Labrador posts such as Northwest River became dependent on so-called Settlers, people of mixed European and Inuit descent, as specialized trappers, while the Innu came to rely on fur trapping more as a supplement to their subsistence hunting economy. The Innu began to feel pressured by the activities of the Settlers when the latter began trapping far in the interior, starting about 1910, although there was sufficient land for the Innu to avoid them most of the time. This competitive pressure ended in 1942 with the establishment of the Goose Bay airbase, as Settler trappers were drawn away to the chance of employment, leaving the Innu in control of the interior.

At first the impact of the Goose Bay base on the Innu was only indirect; the population concentration resulting from the base seriously reduced the game supply on which the Innu depended when they were in the region (Bergerud 1967). Later forestry and roadbuilding activities in the Goose Bay region further reduced this supply. The rapid end to the isolation of the Innu involved two major developments in the Labrador interior: the opening in the 1950s of the iron ore mines of Schefferville, Wabush, and Labrador City, followed by the flooding of the Churchill Falls hydroelectric reservoir (Smith 1975). These developments led to a slowly expanding trans-Labrador road system, as well as to a network of tourist and fishing camps, which together drew more and more non-Innu into the interior.

Apart from the relative lateness of these incursions into Innu lands, compared with those of most other Canadian aboriginal groups, a further aspect to their recent isolation was the lack of an administrative infrastructure specifically devoted to them or oriented to their interests. Prior to its entry into Confederation, Newfoundland had no distinct administration for aboriginal peoples, leaving such matters largely in the hands of missionaries and a police force, the Rangers. Like the fur traders, the Roman Catholic missionaries from the St Lawrence who had originally converted the Innu were seldom able to pay much attention to those of them living in the interior and did not establish themselves year-round at the posts in Labrador until the

1950s, due at first to the Protestant leanings of the Hudson's Bay Company and later to an ecclesiastical jurisdictional dispute (Tanner 1976).

With Confederation looming, an understanding was arrived at between Newfoundland and Canada that the federal government would be responsible for indigenous people living in the new province, in the same way that it was in the rest of Canada. However, the first premier, Joseph Smallwood, apparently had second thoughts when the time came to finalize the terms of entry, while the federal side did not object to leaving matters in limbo (Thompkins 1988). The matter remained unresolved for many years, until the federal government entered what become a succession of joint funding arrangements, allowing indigenous people to be directly administered by the province, but at a more meagre level than similar groups elsewhere in Canada (Roach 1992).

The new funding source was enough, however, to allow the province to quite suddenly bring an end to Innu nomadic autonomy. In the mid-1960s houses and schools were built by the province for the Innu, first at Northwest River and then at Davis Inlet, social assistance payments were started, and various kinds of economic development schemes were experimented with. Innu parents found themselves forced to remain in the communities to send their children to school throughout the winter under threat of losing their social assistance payments. Game laws were for the first time applied to Innu subsistence hunters. By the mid-1970s, when my own work in the region began, the Innu told me they felt that their way of life was under direct attack by the provincial government, whose policies were holding them in the communities and preventing them from practising their hunting way of life.

INNU SOCIAL ISOLATION

The third factor I wish to consider as influencing the adoption of a radical ethnonationalist position is the form of any social relations that exist between the ethnic group in question and other groups in society. In the case of the Labrador Innu, this can best be described as a situation of extreme social isolation.

In summary form, here are the main historical and cultural factors which account for the lack of development of any significant pattern of structured social relations between the Innu and other Labradorians.

1 The Innu were interior dwellers, in contrast to coastal-oriented Inuit and Settlers, and they were rarely seen by the latter except during their short trading visits. The Innu had a nomadic land-tenure system, with subgroups who had a general association with particular regions of the territory, but between which there was continual mobility (Maillot 1986). This fluid pattern conflicted with the permanent residences and fixed traplines of the Settlers. The Innu became largely replaced by Settlers as the main source of furs for the posts, so that even the limited links they had with the traders became attenuated.

2 The Innu were first christianized by Roman Catholic missionaries and through this connection they were influenced by the French. Both of these factors tended to further isolate them from the emerging, predominantly Protestant, civil society of late nineteenth- and early twentieth-century Labrador (Tanner 1976). Yet at the same time their contact with the Roman Catholic church was mostly fleeting, since missionaries only began to reside in Labrador from the 1950s.

3 At brief encounters in the interior some of their relations with individual Settlers were friendly, but there were several hostile incidents, because the Innu resented the Settlers taking their best trapping lands. In contrast to the pattern of relations which developed between Europeans and the Inuit, no intermarriages between Innu and Settlers occurred. The uncompromising Innu values and often sharp-edged Innu personality were found by Europeans to be in marked contrast to those of the more pliant and accommodating Inuit, to whom they had first become adapted. Unlike the Inuit, the Innu did not quickly incorporate the concepts of private property; for example, they did not cash in on the employment opportunity offered by the first Goose Bay base in 1942. Because Innu society was generally equalitarian they were unwilling to act as the social inferiors of the Settlers.

4 The 1927 Labrador boundary decision, and the increasing division of jurisdiction over the Innu between Quebec and Newfoundland, has gradually imposed itself on Innu on either side of the border. Prior to 1927 Newfoundland had effectively disowned the Innu as a whole, treating them as 'Canadian Indians.' This can be illustrated in the way those who arrived at a post in Labrador in a starving condition were treated. In contrast to how the Newfoundland government dealt with any Inuit or Settlers, if welfare rations had to be issued to any Innu, the cost was charged to the Canadian

government. This practice changed after 1927. However, the border still means more to non-Innu than it does to the Innu. The Sheshat-shit Innu group still see themselves at the centre of a hub of Innu communities, having ties to all other communities to the south, west, and north, most of which happen to be in Quebec. Their particular concern is more with Innu unity, than it is with their Labrador, as opposed to a Quebec, identity.

5   There is little in the way of established administrative structures to handle relations between the Innu and the provincial government. Before Confederation, informal Settler 'laws,' which had no official standing, were given priority by Labrador magistrates, when Set-tlers came into conflict with the Innu (Tanner 1976). After Confed-eration, a weak provincial government administrative system dealing with relations with indigenous people was established, but it has always been more oriented toward the Inuit, in part because the Innu are considered as difficult to deal with by the civil ser-vants concerned.

6   The social isolation of the Innu has now become self-perpetuating. Ethnonationalist policies have resulted in an intensification of their social isolation, because of the resentment other Labradorians have for their political activities. This confirms Innu perceptions that their strategy of asserting themselves as an autonomous people, surrounded by hostile society of which they are not a part, makes good sense.

CONCLUSION

All indigenous groups living within nation-states formulate some of their political arguments on the basis of the assertion of ethnic nationalism. Many of these arguments are directed against the state itself. However, if we examine political actions as well as political ideology, a wide variation can be seen in the degree to which such groups are willing to offer a fundamental challenge to the authority of the state and are willing to act on the basis of such a challenge.

In this paper I have examined how the Innu, and in particular the Innu of Sheshatshit, Labrador, have over the past twenty years adopted an uncompromising ideology and an ethnonationalist pro-gram. I have argued that by looking at the particularities of their situation, their history, their culture, the threats to their present way of life, and the marginal and insecure position they have within the wider society, we can better understand why they have adopted this relatively extreme form of ethnic nationalism, as compared with those of other Canadian indigenous groups.

My explanation has focused in particular on the impact of the relatively recent and rapid decline in the autonomy of the Labrador Innu and on their increasing social isolation. Although they have always been in Labrador, they have effectively been ignored and have become marginalized. They are a people who are, in the context of the majority society that surrounds them, 'hidden in plain sight.' This social marginality can be seen in their relations with governments and other groups in the wider Canadian society, but also and especially within Labrador society which has virtually grown up around them, but which has failed to find a satisfactory place for them. To convey their concerns from within this perceived situation of isolation has led them to adopt more and more strident and extreme forms of communication in their attempt to be listened to and to be taken seriously.

Acknowledgments

My thanks to the Innu people of Sheshatshit, Labrador, for giving me access to their ideas, even though they are far more capable of representing them than I am. The paper has also benefitted with both factual details and insights by Peter Armitage, who is, of course, not responsible for how I have used them. Funding for research in Sheshatshit over the years has been gratefully received from the Institute of Social and Economic Research, Memorial University, the Naskapi Montagnais Innu Association and, most recently, the Social Sciences and Humanities Research Council of Canada.

NOTES

1 While the majority of the Innu, or Montagnais–Naskapi, reside in Quebec, from Lac St Jean eastward, this paper is concerned mainly with those based in Labrador. The two provincial groups are, socially and culturally, a single people. But each has its own distinct political organization, and each with its own ideological viewpoint. Even the use of indigenous term 'Innu' when using English or French separates them, since it has been promoted by the Labrador group, while the Quebec group continues to use the term 'Montagnais.'

2 Eventually the film became a co-production involving the British group,

Nexus Television, and the National Film Board of Canada, and was entitled 'Hunters and Bombers' (Brody and Markham 1990).
3 This approach was, in fact, successfully taken in the mid-1980s by another Newfoundland aboriginal group, the Micmacs of Conne River.
4 Despite the fact that the Office of Native Claims (ONC) have published maps showing what they consider to be the extent of the Labrador Innu claim, the absence of clear boundaries has recently been used by ONC as a pretext for suggesting that the original claim was incomplete.

REFERENCES

Andrews, Lyla. 1984. 'Kakuspinanut: A Review of the Outpost Programme – Davis Inlet.' Report prepared for the Naskapi Montagnais Innu Association. Happy Valley, Labrador: Innu Ltd.
Armitage, Peter. 1991. *The Innu (The Montagnais–Naskapi)* New York: Chelsea House
– Armitage, Peter, and John Kennedy. 1989. 'Redbaiting and Racism on our Frontier: Military Expansion in Labrador and Quebec.' *Canadian Review of Sociology and Anthropology* 26(5): 799–817
Bergerud, A.T. 1967. 'Management of Labrador Caribou.' *Journal of Wildlife Management* 31: 621–42
Beyer Broch, Harald. 1983. 'The Bluefish River Incident,' in A. Tanner (ed.), *The Politics of Indianness.* St John's: Institute of Social and Economic Research, pp. 137–96
Brody, Hugh, and Nigel Markham (directors). 1990. *Hunters and Bombers* (documentary film). London: Nexus Television and Montreal: National Film Board of Canada
Charest, Paul. 1983. 'Hydroelectric Dam Construction and the Foraging Activities of Eastern Quebec Montagnais,' in E. Leacock and R.B. Lee (eds.), *Politics and History in Band Societies.* Cambridge: Cambridge University Press, pp. 413–26
Connor, Walker. 1973. 'The Politics of Ethnonationalism.' *Journal of International Affairs* 21(1): 1–21
Government of Newfoundland. 1984. 'Sheshatshit Innu Council Outpost Programme Cost-Effectiveness Analysis, July.' Report prepared for the Rural, Agricultural and Northern Development Department, Government of Newfoundland. St John's: Gardner and Coombs
Grant, Hugh. 1981. 'The Exploitation of Natural Resources in Ntesinan: Estimates of Past and Future Rents.' Reports prepared for the Naskapi–Montagnais Innu Association, Sheshatshiu, Labrador
La Rusic, I.R. et al. 1979. *Negotiating a Way of Life. Initial Cree Experience*

with the Administrative Structures of the James Bay Agreement. Ottawa: Department of Indian Affairs and Northern Development

Maillot, José. 1986. 'Territorial Mobility among the Montagnais–Naskapi of Labrador.' *Anthropologica* n.s. 18(1-2): 92–107

Parkin, David. 1978. *The Cultural Definition of Political Response.* New York: Academic Press

Ponting, J. Rick, and Roger Gibbings. 1980. *Out of Irrelevance.* Toronto: Butterworths

Roach, James. 1992. 'Canada–Newfoundland Agreements. An Innu Perspective.' Report written for the Innu Nation, Sheshatshit, Labrador

Savard, Rémi. 1979. *Destins d'Amérique. Les Autochtones et Nous.* Montreal: L'hexagone

Smith, Philip. 1975. *Brinco: The Story of Churchill Falls.* Toronto: McClelland and Stewart

Tanner, Adrian. 1976. Land Use and Land Tenure of the Indians of Southern Labrador. Report for Naskapi–Montagnais Innu Association, Sheshatshit, Labrador

– 1983a. 'Introduction: The Politics of Dependency,' in Tanner (ed.), *The Politics of Indianness.* St John's: Institute of Social and Economic Research

– 1983b. 'Algonquian Land Tenure and State Structures in the North.' *Canadian Journal of Native Studies* 3(2): 311–20

– and Peter Armitage. 1986. *Native Resource Use Study, Environmental Impact Assessment, Ross Bay Junction–Churchill Falls Tote Road.* Environmental Assessment Report, Department of Transporation, Government of Newfoundland. St John's: Hardy and Associates

– and Sakej Henderson. 1992. 'Aboriginal Land Claims in the Atlantic Provinces,' in K. Coates (ed.), *Aboriginal Land Claims in Canada.* Toronto: Copp Clark Pittman

Thompkins, Edward. 1988. 'Pencilled Out: Newfoundland and Labrador's Native People and Canadian Confederation, 1947–1954' A report prepared for Jack Harris, M.P. Ottawa, House of Commons

Wadden, Marie. 1991. *Nitassinan. The Innu Struggle to Reclaim their Homeland.* Vancouver: Douglas and McIntyre

recognized that both history and identity are as much mental constructs as positivistic or demonstrable facts 'out there,' allowing for frequent and subtle shifts in both dimensions where necessary. The main principle is that the two be mutually supporting and consistent, even in the face of contradictory historiographical 'facts.' The ideas that perceptions of the past are constantly reshaped by the present status quo and that a replication of current ideals is commonly projected onto past time have received considerable attention by anthropological disciples of the social historian Hobsbawm (cf. Hobsbawm and Ranger 1983), and are particularly appropriate and pressing in the domain of ethnic studies.

Academic observers, as much as participants in 'real' ethnic or nationalistic events, have long appreciated the importance of origins and antiquity as values in themselves, as well as the basis for claims and counter-claims. They give rise to many related metaphors having to do with 'roots,' ancestors, first or original peoples and nations, homelands, sacred burial sites and, 'tradition' generally, as Canada's Native peoples have recently used to considerable effect. Often the myth alone is sufficient but where appropriate, further hard evidence may be sought by calling into service archaeological or other corroborating sources, as in the case of the Biblical holy lands for Israel or the ancient sites of certain kingdoms for West African states.

The quality of indigenousness or aboriginality is a resurgent one in today's world, whether in ex-colonial territories of the Third World, in amalgamated empires such as the former Soviet Union, or in the growing number of multi-ethnic or plural immigrant-settler states, as represented by Canada. In such states citizenship is acquired by birth within the territory or by naturalization, but this bears no relationship to generational depth of residence or association, nor yet to any sense of indigenousness or founding status. The connotation of a people or ethnic group, however, confers a power and identity generally more compelling than that of citizenship alone, for it is only in the rarest of cases where all citizens are of a single ethnic origin in the form of a true 'nation-state,' popular usage notwithstanding. In some multi-ethnic states, it is the goal of some citizens to legitimate, entrench, or to regain lost privileges and status over other citizens by reference to the myth of indigenousness, particularly in the context of domestic politics. Loss of indigenous status as a 'founding people,' can result from engulfment by other immigrants, by voluntary migration to a new host country, and status demotion from a position of national dominance in an original homeland, or by conquest by an alien power. Today's 'Fourth World' peoples base their claims and grievances on an ancestral heritage antedating that of all their fellow-citizens in the states into which they have become incorporated (and subordinated). However, by pressing these internal issues beyond the domestic level and onto a world stage, they are perforce led inexorably into the second level required of a successful modern national movement, that involving an international image and recognition, which in turn helps to feed their credibility at home. The status of indigenousness has received differing treatment in constitutional and legal systems around the world, but in most of the New World (of the Americas), including Canada, the Native population has succumbed to a situation of migrant superordination, legally, constitutionally, and socially. In another kind of situation, however, it is an already resident population which attempts to control and defend its dominant position, politically, constitutionally, and culturally, against immigrant newcomers, by imposing strict constraints on the terms of citizenship, immigration, and national culture. Malaysia is such a state, where the Malays, for whom the country is named, resolutely defend their political and cultural advantages over the 'immigrant' populations who collectively make up a 'minority' perilously close to 50 per cent of the total.

MALAYSIA AS A MULTI-ETHNIC STATE

Under British colonial influence, beginning in the late eighteenth century and ending with independence in 1957, substantial adjustments to the local population, as well as political and economic structures were effected. First, the nine original independent Malay sultanates on the peninsula gradually acquired a sense of common identity superseding their original political borders, which ultimately, in a more evolved form, became the underpinning of a political activism uniting the Malays of the entire peninsula against all non-Malay immigrants. Such a level of unity had no precedent in any royal or military alliance in known precolonial history, when 'Malayness' did not transcend the boundaries of a sultanate or loyalties to the individual ruler. The post-independence solution to a surplus of sultans and a counter to any tendency to separatism along such lines was to implement a unique system 'rotating kingship,' whereby the king of Malaysia is selected sequentially from each original sultanate in turn every five years. This made the expression of a pan-Malay unity administratively feasible. At the same time, provision was made for the administration of Islam through the Shari'ah courts locally, with the sultans as ultimate arbiters of 'Malay religion and custom,' which helped to preserve their symbolic importance to the Malay population and entrenched the connection between Malayness and Islam (Hooker 1983; Yegar 1984) – to the exclusion of other, non-Malay, Muslims on the peninsula. This marked the beginning of the 'ethnicization' of Islam in the country. Finally, the Malay language, the official language of the post-independence state, appropriated what had long been a trading lingua franca in the coastal parts of the region now known as Indonesia and Malaysia, and made suitable, with some circumlocutory adjustments, for administrative and bureaucratic functions.

During their occupancy and economic exploitation of the peninsula, the British found it expedient to import substantial cohorts of Indian indentured labourers for the plantations, while even larger numbers of Chinese were encouraged to take advantage and considerable control of mining and commercial urban activities. The assumption by the British was that the Malays had little inclination or cultural preparation for any economic role other than as a rice-growing peasantry. In this they were encouraged by the setting aside of reservation lands, from the earliest part of the twentieth century, lands which still remain immune from purchase or alienation to non-Malays. Thus, the crystallization and feasibility of the idea of 'Malayness' as an identity and as an ethnic 'reality,' began as a consequence of colonial policy arrangements, including the re-arrangement of peoples within the colonial domain. This legacy continues as an embodiment of emergent nationalism in a framework of differential ethnic statuses, and in the concept of a 'founding nation' among the populations of the peninsula.

ETHNICITY AND THE CONSTITUTION

During the 1940s and 1950s, with the approach to independence, the proportion of the collective immigrant population almost matched that of the Malays. At the time, the censuses for the peninsula (now West Malaysia) record a total of only forty-eight per cent Malays, with thirty-seven per cent Chinese, and ten per cent Indians. The balance of 'others' included about one per cent of forest-dwelling, nomadic 'tribal' peoples, who revealingly, are known locally as the 'original' or 'indigenous' people (*orang asli*). Subsequently, in 1963,

North Borneo joined the political union to create the Federation of Malaysia, thereby adding a further seven per cent of aboriginal or *orang asli* populations and swelling their proportion in the population of the country as a whole.

Meanwhile, on the political front, a series of acrimonious debates preceded British withdrawal, beginning with the Malayan Union (1946–48), in which the eventual legal and constitutional status, including citizenship, of the respective populations was at issue (Stockwell 1979; Stenson 1980). The eventual result at independence in 1957 was the framing of a constitution whereby the Malays acquired the official status of what Canadians would understand as a charter or founding nation, a form of first class citizenship which confers upon them the unique prerogative of providing the prime minister of the country (as well as the constitutional monarch), accompanied by an assortment of quotas favouring the Malays in high-level civil service positions and access to other desirable resources. Malay cultural dominance was also affirmed in the primacy accorded to the Malay language and custom, with Islam as the official religion, and the recognition of the Malay sultans as their protectors. These privileges and advantages were elaborated and extended following the introduction of the Second Malaysia Plan and the New Economic Policy of 1971 in the form of affirmative educational, occupational, and other economic quotas. The New Economic Policy set in motion a restructuring of the Malaysian economy, with the goal of retrieving some of the perceived lost ground in modern, urban, professional, and commercial sectors from the Chinese and Indians, now referred to as 'immigrants' (*kaum pendatang*). This affirmative action policy is still in effect and, as of 1990, has been renewed in substantially the same form.

In light of the politico-economic base of the Malaysian state, it is apparent that a crucial concern for Malaysians is the question as to who is in fact eligible for these special privileges, i.e., who is a real Malay? To this question, the state, by its 1957 constitution, provides a formula. By its standards, a 'Malay' is one who speaks the Malay language, practises (an unspecified amount of) Malay custom, is a Muslim, and the subject of a Malay sultan by virtue of birth and residence in a Malay state. What was not anticipated, but quickly realized, however, is that this is essentially a cultural definition of identity or ethnicity, opening up the possibility of assimilation to Malayness, by learning the language and a modicum of customs and by conversion to Islam, for anyone born locally. The logical consequence was that assimilation, if pursued by substantial numbers, could ultimately defeat the entire spirit and purpose of the constitution. Furthermore, the legal codification of ethnic status locked the Malays into a defensive position, against what are (legally) well-founded claims by assimilated non-Malay Malaysians with converging or conflicting interests in economic and political resources, when judged by more universalistic standards. In fact, today, most younger Malaysians have been through their entire educational career in the Malay language, are familiar with as many Malay customs as are most of the westernized Malay elites, and, as will be seen, have sometimes converted to Islam. But in official policy, all Malaysian citizens remain locked into their ancestral ethnic category, which is inscribed on their identity cards and continues to influence much of their public life.

Neither Malaya in 1957 nor Malaysia today has ever seriously entertained the idea of assimilation for its immigrants, remaining a defiantly plural state. Since independence, it has officially 'frozen' immigration, both in principle, in support of its opposition to any characterization as an 'immigrant society,' but more particularly and practically, to prevent any further increase in an already alarming proportion of 'minorities' to threaten Malay status in their own country. This was one of the many reasons why the Malaysian authorities so forcefully rejected the supplicant 'boat-people' from Indochina (many of whom were reputedly ethnic Chinese). What it less well known, however, is that a number of refugee Cham people, a minority Muslim population from Cambodia, allegedly with distant relations to the Malays, were discreetly permitted to settle.[1]

Finally, the above constitutional arrangements received their institutional consummation in the form of separate 'ethnic' political parties. The Malays were represented by their United Malays National Organization (UMNO) which had germinated in the days immediately prior to independence, constitutionally the senior partner in a political alliance whose junior members were the Malaysian Chinese Association (MCA) and the Malaysian Indian Congress (MIC). Even more to the point is that party affiliation cannot be changed, but must always correspond with the appropriate 'ethnicity.'

THE MYTH OF THE BUMIPUTERA

Over the years, a series of strategies and rationales have been designed to defend Malay privileges and to maintain boundaries between Malays and non-Malays. One of these is the cultivation of the myth of indigenousness and its perpetuation vis-à-vis 'immigration' from generation to generation. This concept, known as the Bumiputera (Sanskrit for 'sons, or princes, of the soil') has had a diffuse and imprecise currency in the Malay language as a general way of expressing ideas of indigeneity, since at least the early part of the twentieth century. Now, however, it has been resurrected in the form of a union between Malays and the *orang asli* and endowed with a new legal and political significance and the source of much political rhetoric (Chandra 1985).

As it happens, however, this solution too has led to unexpected problems and confusion. For while the *orang asli* enjoy undisputable credibility as natives or indigenes, they cannot qualify as 'Malays' on constitutional grounds, since most of them are not Muslim, and few are willing to convert. Furthermore, when 'Bumiputeraism' first was made a legal category, it was not seriously anticipated that the non-Malay Bumiputera would ever make any political claims or engage in political party activities in their own right. Certainly it was tacitly assumed that any political participation by the latter would automatically be channelled through the UMNO, an assumption first challenged in the late 1980s in some assertively independent political activities by non-Malay Bumiputera in the East Malaysian state of Sabah. Despite these problems, however, the Bumiputera idea fulfilled one of its other principal functions in helping to propel the non-immigrant census statistics above the psychologically critical level of 50 per cent. As of 1980, the census records a total of 55.3 per cent Malays/Bumiputera, 33.8 per cent Chinese, 10.2 per cent Indian, and 0.7 per cent Other.

Given the preoccupation with the indigenous ideal and with the 'numbers game' that has accompanied it, it is not altogether surprising that of late a growing cohort of technically illegal immigrants from the islands of Indonesia in search of employment has managed to slip through the official net and avoid public acknowledgment. This tacit acceptance harks back to an earlier, precolonial concept of a generalized cultural area spanning the entire Indonesian archipelago and the Malay peninsula, variously called *Nusantara* or *Melayu Raya*, a 'greater Malay world' (Rustum 1976). As in Malaya/Malaysia, postcolonial state formation processes in Indonesia have artificially welded together an assortment of erstwhile distinctly labelled groups (e.g., Javanese, Sundanese, Acehnese, Balinese) into a common category in opposition to the (mostly Chinese) immigrants, and here known as the *Pribumi*, Indonesia's counterpart to the Bumiputera. In Indonesia too a national language has been created from the old Malay trading lingua franca, and most of the Pribumi are officially Muslim. All of this helps to explain the toleration and covert absorption of these illegal migrants in Malaysia, in addition to their needed economic contributions as menial labourers and domestics. It also explains the seeming paradox that illegal Filipino immigrants (particularly to Sabah in East Malaysia), who fill identical economic niches and functions, are a constant source of irritation to the authorities who attempt to eject and repatriate them when discovered. Once again, it must be assumed that these contradictory immigration practices occur in part for their ultimate effect in improving the demographic balance between Bumiputera and other populations, whether recent immigrants or not.

Once again, this raises a paradox. It is a well-known historiographical fact, if not always part of the public myth, that many present-day Malays, although born in Malaysia, in fact have but shallow genealogical roots on the peninsula. Indeed, in private, many will freely acknowledge that their grandparents came from 'somewhere else,' usually one of the same Indonesian islands as the contemporary illegals. Many modern Malays too still recognize Indonesian kin across the Straits of Malacca. This view of indigeneousness is one in which the modern state intervenes, fracturing the Bumiputera/Pribumi along the lines of modern political units.

A further irony arises when it is recognized that there remains in Malaysia a substantial constituency of 'old' Chinese and Indian families whose residence on the Malay peninsula has greater generational depth than that of some Malays. The so-called Baba Chinese community, for example, can demonstrate a continuous settlement for over three centuries, during which time some of them adopted a habitual use of the Malay language and many domestic customs (Tan 1988). Likewise, a number of Indian merchant families can trace a history of several generations on the peninsula, some from the days of the seventeenth-century Malacca mercantile community. Yet these long-settled communities continue to be referred to as *kaum pendatang* or 'immigrants,' while the Malays provide legitimation for their distinctiveness through references to the most famous ancient 'Malay' kingdoms of Majapahit and Malacca as symbols of their ancient rights (Milner 1983). It is apparent that no official or constitutional definition of identity can effectively cover all the contingencies of practical social life and any definition will create certain anomalies

requiring an increasing complex array of amendments and refine-
ments. In this context, the myth of indigenousness remains among
the most powerful.

MALAYNESS AND ISLAM

The other element of dissonance or ambiguity invading the Bumiputera category of course is religion. On the one hand, the unity of
indigenousness is divided into Muslim and non-Muslim varieties,
while on the other, there exists the ever-present possibility that
Malay-speaking non-Malays converting to Islam will wish to claim
their constitutional 'due.' Once again, it is worth recalling that in
earlier centuries prior to formal colonialism and a modern state, it
had been customary for converts to Islam to be popularly regarded
as 'Malay,' where the local adage equated entering Islam and becoming Malay (*masuk Islam, masuk Melayu*). Following 1957, however, the
logic of attempting the Islamic route to Malayness (and its privileges)
was indeed tested. During the 1970s in particular, when the New
Economic Policy came into effect, a number of unemployed Chinese
males, with their sights apparently set upon certain goals of employment, training schemes, licences, and loans normally reserved for
Malays, did in fact convert to Islam. At this time considerable ambiguity still existed in official circles as to the status of these converts.
Throughout the 1970s, debates stirred in bureaucratic agencies and
even Parliament as to whether such individuals should be considered
as 'Malays,' as to whether they should change their names from
Chinese to Arabic ('Malay') ones, and indeed whether a change of
ethnic status should be recorded on their identity cards (Nagata
1978). Whereas the families of many of the Chinese converts often
assumed that the latter had 'become/gone over to, the Malays,' and
they were often socially rejected on these grounds by their community, they were rarely fully accepted socially by the Malays, but were
relegated to a specially created marginal category of 'new associates'
in Islam (*saudara baru*). This accorded the converts status as fellows
in the faith, but not as co-ethnics. All the converts' religious activities
were overseen by a Chinese Muslim association, which controlled the
circumstances of their interaction with Malays and kept them as
religious marginals. As the number of converts increased during the
1970s, however, any tentative goodwill or ritual acceptance began to
evaporate, and the continuing ethnic separateness of the Chinese
Muslims was affirmed, thus avoiding the inevitable economic conse-

quences of their assimilation as Malays. Subsequently, and particularly under the influence of more recent Islamic resurgence, a situation
of increasing alienation of polarization has developed between Chinese and Malays, and there has been considerable recidivism among
the ranks of the 'new associates,' while the Chinese Muslim association is now defunct.

There are of course in Malaysia other non-Malay Muslims, in
addition to Indonesian Pribumi and Chinese converts. In the case of
Indian Muslims with a long and respectable Islamic pedigree, it
might be anticipated that acceptance into the Malay fold would be
rather more easily achieved. Yet even here recognition and sentiment
of a separate, immigrant origin often intrudes. It is true that some
Indians have managed to slip through the net, as have some Indian
businessmen needing certain 'Malay' licences or contacts and, in such
cases, have even moved from the Indian to the Malay Chamber of
Commerce. In most cases, however, they are identified and on occasion even stigmatized by a derogatory epithet connoting either a
separate (and undesirable) or hybrid ancestry, e.g., Jawi Peranakan
(implying a local-born foreigner), while the rather coarse terms
Mamak and Kling are used for Malaysian Indian Muslims. In practice, most Indian Muslims prefer to maintain separate mosques and
religious associations and also to remain loyal to the Indian political
party, the MIC.

Beginning in the 1970s further, the saga of Malay identity took
another turn, in the direction of greater identification with Islam and
the Muslim resurgence. Overseas educational and occupational opportunities (among the perquisites of Malay ethnic status), had
exposed local Malays to contacts and influences with Muslims from
the other parts of the world, particularly from the Islamic core areas
of the Middle East. As a result, many of the revivalist ideas there
current, and as particularly embodied in the Iranian revolution, were
brought back to Malaysia by the expatriates to receptive students and
colleagues at home. Having lost the distinctive boundaries of language and custom, and hoisted on the uncertain petard of Bumiputeraism, attention was concentrated on the one remaining element of
Malay identity, Islam. At this point local and international interests
came together. This had the effect of demonstrating to the Malays the
existence of another significant audience in the world beyond
Malaysia. Increasingly, in this world of international communications,
diaspora, and expatriate communities, peoples are becoming aware
of their image on a world stage and of their membership in commun-

ities beyond the state. In the case of the Malays, this identity focuses on the international Muslim community (*ummat*), whence it draws another source of legitimacy. In keeping with this latest emphasis on Islam, some new interpretations of Malay history have begun increasingly to locate its people in an Islamic universe, over and above one of Nusantara or local indigeneity. Over the past two decades, the Malaysian Historical Society has issued a series of publications concentrating on the legacy of Islam in all facets of local life. An earlier, historiographically and archaeologically demonstrated substratum of Indic and other pre-Islamic local custom has been subordinated to the saga of the planting of the Muslim faith and on tales of migration and contact with the Middle East and Muslim parts of South Asia. Where possible, Arab connections and genealogies are discovered, together with other links between Malay mosques, religious schools, tombs of holy men, and places in the Islamic heartland. This sacralization of Malay history transcends the Southeast Asian region, replacing it with a sacred geography which gives Malays a more global role and identity, a new cachet for a people hitherto little known outside its region. The paradox in this latest development in Malay identity is that to its domestic audience Islam is a jealously guarded Malay prerogative, whereby a common faith is divided along ethnic lines, while in the international sphere Malayness derives a new dimension from its association and identification with Muslims of other ethnic and national groups sharing a universal religious character and culture. Thus, the local and international character of Malayness takes on different forms and expressions. This distinction is highlighted even more graphically in the character of the recently established International Islamic University in Malaysia, which as its name implies, draws students from across the Muslim world. In contrast to other Malaysian universities, where the national (Malay) language is assertively imposed, the Islamic University freely uses English and Arabic, while the social interaction of Muslims of many nationalities makes the absence of any sense of confraternity among local Malaysian Muslims all the more remarkable. Further, what are forms of Muslim dress in the international community (such as variants of a head veil and a long, body-obscuring robe for women) have become, in Malaysia, as much a symbol of Malay ethnic identity, an ethnic costume distinguishing individuals effectively and unambiguously in a multi-cultural public.[2]

The lack of total correspondence between the transnational and the local images and strategies of Malayness relate very much to a perception of a place in a wider scheme. When this wider scheme is still domestic, and considerations of Malay hegemony are paramount, any commonality which could be squeezed from the sharing of a faith or of birthplace, language, or custom must be zealously kept from intruding into the privileged domain. Hence the utility of the concept of indigenousness and the appropriate mythical armamentarium to make it more convincing and compelling. When, however, the focus shifts to a more international context, different parameters are more effective in conferring a meaningful status and recognition to a relatively minor people, and these centre on the community of Muslims. In this world, the notion of indigenousness or Bumiputera has little significance.

CONCLUSIONS

The recent history of postcolonial, multiethnic Malaysia provides a clear illustration of the role and power of the state, together with its legal and constitutional apparatus, in creating, shaping, sustaining, and containing ethnic identities, sentiments, and expressions. It also illuminates the process whereby one people among many, the Malays, has achieved a special status as a 'founding nation' with a charter of indigenousness as a basis for political and economic privileges. This brings to mind comparable circumstances in contemporary Canada. Like Canada, Malaysia tries to manage the paradox of fostering 'national unity' (i.e., state unity), while keeping its ethnic communities distinct, and in some situations, following discriminatory 'affirmative'-action-like policies for some of its citizens, in what Kuper and Smith (1969) calls 'differential incorporation' as a form of structural pluralism.

Unlike Canada, however, in Malaysia it is the indigenous population, under its Bumiputera designation, which is dominant and which maintains its dominance as controller of the state and as gatekeeper of immigration. However, in the very process of codification of (Malay) identity, the Malaysian state has unwittingly exposed itself to the 'dangers' of assimilation, hence loss of privilege, from which it has tried to extricate itself by a confusing series of amendments, such as the Bumiputera revision. In any case, these shifts underscore the multifaceted and changing bases of ethnic identities, which permit conflicts between ideas of indigenousness and religion as effective boundaries. These emerge even more starkly in the international context, where Malays acquire world status and recognition by means of association across ethnic lines with fellow Muslims, whereas in their homeland they allow ethnic division to intrude upon any religious unity. In the modern world of transnational communities, such 'two-faced' or discrepant images or expressions of identity should probably be expected to become more common, given the differing interests in the two domains, and this may emerge in the behaviours of Native peoples in such countries as Canada in contrast to their activities in international Fourth World movements.

Finally, such cautionary tales should be borne in mind in the event that any legal codification of the meaning of 'Quebecois' in an independent Quebec ever be contemplated as a basis for special status. Were such a status to be defined in terms of specific parameters such as language, birthplace, and possibly religion, for example, any special privileges would be hard to defend beyond a second-generation immigrant population. If more narrowly restricted to those of a particular 'origin' or 'race,' e.g., those of French descent or origin, this would invite other forms of legal response, on the grounds of discrimination or violation of the charter of human rights, thus setting two principles, one universalist and one ethnonationalist, in direct confrontation. It could even be envisaged that, were the Quebecois to interpret the idea of indigenousness in their province too zealously, they too could face an internal contradiction not unlike that of the Bumiputera of Malaysia.

NOTES

1 In 1992, the country's gates were generously opened to over a hundred Bosnian 'Muslims' from distant Europe.
2 In the new world order following the disintegration of the Soviet Union, one of the prongs of Malaysia's foreign policy has been to pursue an alignment of new Muslim states, such as Uzbekhistan and Kazakhstan, where it hopes to play a leadership role, and add greater strength to the world of Islamic community. In this sacred political geography, the Malays are once again seeking global recognition.

REFERENCES

Chandra, Muzaffar. 1985. 'Malayism, Bumiputeraism and Islam,' in A. Ibrahim. S. Siddique, and Y. Hussein (eds.), *Readings on Southeast Asian Islam*. Singapore: Institute of Southeast Asian Studies, pp. 356–61
Hobsbawm, E., and T. Ranger (eds.). 1983. *The Invention of Tradition*. Cambridge: Cambridge University Press

Hooker, M.B. 1983. 'Muhammadan Law and Islamic Law,' in M.B. Hooker (ed.), *Islam in Southeast Asia*. Leiden: Brill, pp. 160–82

Kuper, Leo, and M.G. Smith (eds.). 1969. *Pluralism in Africa*. Berkeley and Los Angeles: University of California Press

Milner, A. 1982. *Kerajaan: Malay Political Culture on the Eve of Colonial Rule.* St. Lucia: University of Queensland Press

Nagata, Judith. 1978. 'The Chinese Muslims of Malaysia: New Malays or New Associates? A Problem in Ethnicity,' in G. Means (ed.), *The Past in Southeast Asia's Present*. Selections from the Proceedings of the Canadian Council of Southeast Asian Studies, 1977, pp. 102–27

– 1984. *The Reflowering of Malaysian Islam: From Peasant Roots to Religious Radicals*. Vancouver. University of British Columbia Press

Rustum, Sani. 1976. 'Malaya Raya as a Malay Nation of Intent,' in H.M. Dahlan (ed.), *The Nascent Malaysian Society*: Kebangsaan University Malaysia: Siri Monograf Jabatan Sosiologi dan Antropologi

Stenson, Michael. 1980. *Race, Class and Colonialism in West Malaysia*. St. Lucia: University of Queensland Press

Stockwell, A.J. 1979. *British Policy and Malay Politics during the Malayan Union Experiment, 1942–1948*. Kuala Lumpur: Malayan Branch of the Royal Asiatic Society, Monograph No. 8

Tan, Chee Beng. 1988. *The Baba of Malacca: Culture and Identity of a Chinese Peranakan Community in Malaysia*. Petaling Jaya: Pelanduk Publications

Yegar, Moshe. 1984. 'The Development of Islamic Institutional Structure in Malaya, 1987–1941: The Impact of British Administrative Reforms,' in R. Israeli and A. Johns (eds.), *Islam in Asia*, vol. 2. Boulder, Colo.: Westview Press

 CHAPTER 6

Ethnic Profile, Historical Processes, and the Cultural Identity Crisis among Quebeckers of French Descent

Marc-Adélard Tremblay

CULTURAL IDENTITY AND DEVELOPMENT

The idea of making an ethnological analysis of the cultural identity crisis among Quebeckers of French descent seems to be well suited for a colloquium entitled 'Ethnonationalism: Canadian and International Perspective.' I want to do it from a development perspective. The close relationships that exist between cultural identity and societal development are of such importance that they justify both the nature and the orientations of such a theoretical stand. Some of these justifications are, from the standpoint of the vital interests of a particular ethnic group, related to the concept of its development (or of its social progress) and to the imperative, of its 'culturalization.' Others refer to social conditions that make development possible through a process of self-consciousness on the part of the whole ethnic group. Whereas the former belong to the order of objectives, the latter are integral parts of instrumental strategies.

The social progress of an ethnic group can be slowed down or accelerated by a large number of sociopolitical and sociocultural conditions that acquire great significance for the cultural identity of a people. From my viewpoint, the concept of cultural identity has three major components: a collective self-image which, because of its specificity, confers to a group its distinctive character; social institutions that embody its various elements and its way of life; and a projection into the future which ensures its continuity and its lasting while taking into account the dynamism capable of transforming it. Thus conceived, the cultural identity of an ethnic group constitutes a powerful evolutionary lever that firms up ethnic self-image and constitutes a guiding principle for collective development projects. But, for this connection to take place, principles upon which this identity rests must be known and internalized; their concrete expressions, through their consensual nature, must be found in all social strata, and the prospective views of the ethnic group's future must be convergent. We would then be in a situation where the cultural identity of the group is a vigorous one. A weak cultural identity, however, would manifest itself in acculturated behavioural patterns, in cultural confusion, and, at the extreme, in deculturation phenomena. Such cultural patterns could not serve as the launching grounds for creativity and for the conception of future societal projects. The working hypothesis that I wish to document in this case study on French Quebec, from an emic perspective, is that Quebeckers' of French descent are going through a profound cultural identity crisis that imperils the survival of a francophone cultural entity on the North American continent.

THE CULTURAL IDENTITY CRISIS OF FRENCH-SPEAKING QUEBECKERS

In order to document the hypothesis advanced here, the type of analysis follows two interconnected pathways: that of institutional frameworks and that of the life habits of individuals in their respective sociocultural niches. Such splitting of a pattern is being made with the view to giving a sharper perspective on these two fundamental aspects of the ethnicity crisis of Quebec francophones.

Social Institutions

The cultural identity principles, the particular social institutions as well as the other complementary phenomena tied to ethnicity, from a collective standpoint appear to me to be sharp reading instruments in the examination of the impact of rapid social changes, whether they are the results of endogenous determinants or the consequences of external dynamisms, to the extent that they best reflect the numerous dialectical tensions existing between individual and collective identity, between idiosyncratic behavioural patterns and institutional armatures, and between resistance to change and involvement in acculturational processes. The swing between these polar stances obeys cultural norms and constraints that act either as curbing or pressure elements, as much at the level of the individual in his daily living as that of institutional frameworks. A close examination of these oscillations might lead to discovering how and through which processes they transform the ethnic image that the French-speaking Quebeckers have of themselves as a group, their ways of life, and their social representations that nurture their concepts and views relating to social development (*les projets de société*).

Although they have fostered the use of the French language in public services throughout Canada, federal linguistic policies related to the concept of a multicultural state and the policies on bilingualism – including in this Bill C-72 – have not been successful in stopping the proportional reduction of the francophone population of Canada that has occurred in the past few decades. The French-speaking population of Canada today barely represents twenty-five per cent of the total. In contrast, within the Province of Quebec, the population of French descent has been successful in maintaining its relative numerical importance, eighty per cent of the total population, despite a sharp decrease in the birth rate. Such a stability, however, cannot necessarily be viewed as a marker of the vigour of cultural traditions, since it is being accompanied by the shattering of ethnic institutions and the weakening of the basic principles of the cultural identity configuration (Tremblay 1983).

Let us look at historical processes with the intent of documenting that assertion. The national consciousness of Quebeckers of French descent arose in the middle of the nineteenth century, that is, about one hundred years after the British Conquest. At that time, they collectively became aware that the Roman Catholic church, the parochial confessional school, the patriarchal family, their network of social solidarity, and the French language were the main ethnic institutions of what was then being called the 'French Canadian Nation.' Through that expressed recognition, these social institutions became the armature of cultural patterns that embodied a spiritual worldview, a type of ruralist and theocentric social organization, at the heart of which was an abundant population constituting the main contingent factor for economic production and the reproduction of cultural patterns. A conservative nationalism, self-centred and impervious to external ideologies, was at first an affirmative nationalism and gradually became an aspiration to a nation-state.

At the time of the election of a government led by the Parti Québécois, the distinctive principles of the cultural identity of French-speaking Quebeckers were gradually shifted from ethnic institutions to the nation-state. This transfer in the cultural identity infrastructures brought about some drastic changes in both the content and the expression of Quebec identity. Those changes were so rapid and without due ordering that they fostered many negative consequences. From a nationalistic perspective, one was the discarding, in 1980, of the political sovereignty project.

Far from achieving national aspirations and nurturing collective hopes, the nation-state of French Quebec, at this embryonic stage, was confronted by hard facts in the federal–provincial arena (the repatriation of the Canadian constitution without the consent of Quebec after the negative answer to the Quebec referendum) and by the unpredictable consequences of the 1981–2 economic crisis. These two major events imposed upon the government of René Lévesque the necessity to endorse laws and install administrative policies that were quite unpopular, especially among the most faithful clientele of the Parti Québécois. This conjuncture had given rise to an abrupt disenchantment toward the nation-state, at the same time endangering the cultural foundations of the francophone community. The latter was in such a state of turmoil that it found it impossible to reorient itself on the disintegrating traditional ethnic institutions, nor was it capable of inventing replacement institutions that would be generally attractive. That abrupt discrepancy between French-speaking nationalists and the nation-state happened at the very time when the Quebec spatio-temporal universe was undergoing a massive and undifferentiated invasion by the Anglo-American mass culture. This penetration of southern value systems and models of behaviour has been accentuated by the enforcement in 1989 of free trade policies between Canada and the United States of America which, by the way, do not seem to exclude cultural institutions from the agreement. This dualistic stance, the rejection of the nation-state as a principle of ethnic assertion, on the one hand, and the invasion of public and private life by numerous elements of American culture, on the other, imperceptibly constructed a powerful structure of collective alienation from the original culture.

Some people are going to disagree with me about my statement above. They will use as an argument the established fact that, in the past, French-speaking Quebeckers were successful in surmounting, on a number of occasions, the historical difficulties that became a threat to their ethnicity and that they are still capable, by which *deus ex machina* I do not know, of getting out of the deadlock. Some others, even more optimistic than the preceding ones, reflecting as far as I am concerned a besieged mentality, are going to cast back to the numerous questions associated with the survival of a French Quebec: 'Since our language remains a distinctive cultural trait and continues to be our main instrument for self-affirmation, does it not suffice to convince you'? This powerful linguistic consciousness, to be sure, was attenuated, in its real and symbolic scope, when the Supreme Court of Canada stated that it was unconstitutional to impose French unilingualism in the display of signs outside business establishments. The current government (controlled by the Liberal party), even though it was committed to a federalist ideology, has used the 'notwithstanding' clause in order to enact Bill 178 in the Quebec Legislative Assembly. The bill represents a compromise that has left unsatisfied both the protagonists of a radical nationalism expressed in French unilingualism and the members of the English-speaking community who felt deprived of one of their fundamental individual rights. In general terms, however, Bill 178 has left the great majority of the francophone community satisfied.

That said, it is right to think that Bill 101 produced a strong linguistic consciousness among the intellectual elite and the middle class of the francophone community. But it has failed to francocize immigrants since at present three out of four are English-oriented in order to better their chances of success in the workplace. English is the North American language (*la langue de l'Américanité*), the medium of prestige and of advancement within the professional world. Is it not spoken by more than ninety-five per cent of North American people? It comes as no surprise, then, that French is the only language facing a survival challenge in North America, even in *La Belle Province*. We do not have to be surprised either that Bill 101, until it was rigorously applied, had a limited effect on the process of francocization of business enterprises and of commercial signs and on the improvement of the written and spoken language among members of the upcoming generations.

Furthermore, despite the overwhelming importance of linguistic patterns in a given culture, language only represents one cultural element among many others. To assign to the spoken language the primacy among the foundations of cultural identity, let alone to say that it is the only one, would amount to mistaking the container for the contents. Moreover, to consider the French language in Quebec as a factor of social cohesiveness among French speakers, and between the people of French descent and the various ethnic groups or the indigenous peoples, would amount to giving it a strength that it does not have at this time. Its mediating value and its integrating power are more symbolic than real.

How does one explain this functional weakness of the French language in Quebec? Diverse contextual and conjunctural elements have to be taken into account. Space does not permit a detailed answer, but there is an established fact that is important. The French-speaking community is divided about its main cultural orientations. Value systems of authority, economic standards of living, environmental conditions, ways of life, political affiliation, and so on all vary and, as a result, create many reference points for identity. The diversity of cultural allegiances and ethnic values does not rest on a unitary foundation.

Let me refer to a second category of factors which account for some of the weaknesses of the French language in *La Belle Province* – the cross-cultural context in the school system. In some Montreal schools, for instance, allophone students are more numerous than those of French descent, accentuating the weight of the 'otherness' in systems of thought and in social relationships. It is imperative, too, to underscore the increasing importance of overtly expressed aspirations of the ethnic communities, both old and new, especially in greater Montreal, to participate more actively in the full economic, social, and cultural development of Quebec as full-fledged partners. The leaders of these communities vigorously denounce the social policies of the dominant society aimed at keeping them in a folkloric ghetto. They require, on the basis of sound arguments, an adequate representation in the public and parapublic functions and in the information media. In the workplace, as in daily social environments, they determinedly fight racist prejudices and ethnocentric views of those with whom they interact. To be sure, they live in Quebec but their ethnic roots, their many sources of inspiration and the symbols which express them, while being visible here, especially in the case of ethnic groups having some numerical importance, belong to the mother country. Under all those circumstances, in Metropolitan Montreal at least, the French language is bound to remain at most an instrument of bringing together the French-speaking and those of foreign origin and of reducing areas of misunderstandings. To consider the French language to be a source of social cohesiveness in such a multi-ethnic environment, goes far beyond what it can provide. The functional prerequisites simply do not exist.

*The Sociocultural Universe and the Daily Activities of the
French-speaking in Quebec*

In the first move, I draw a panoramic view of the sociocultural space
of present-day Quebec with the aim of showing the issues at stake
and the various forces acting upon the society. I shall be able, after-
wards, to provide you with the genesis and the evolution of those
issues from the cultural identity standpoint.

Issues at Stake

It appears to me impossible to define the way of life and the daily
activities of French-speaking Quebeckers today without referring to
the settlement patterns along the banks of the St Lawrence River in
the seventeenth century, without reconstructing the main institutional
structures that were responsible for the ways of life and value systems, without alluding to the main dynamics of change that have
been decisive in the evolution of Quebec society toward modernity,
and without identifying the ideological systems that have ensured the
survival of the French culture on the North American continent up
to now. This sketch enables me to outline the profile of institutions,
values, and behaviour of five million French speakers who have built
an original ethnic profile by borrowing cultural elements from three
distinct civilizations: the indigenous peoples (Inuit and Amerindian)
who lived in that territory before the coming of the whites; the settlers originating from numerous French provinces at the beginning
of the seventeenth century who strove to maintain their regional
traditions on American soil; and the various Anglo-Saxon stocks,
settling here after the conquest of Canada by the British in 1760 and
during the decade that followed the American Revolution (1775–85),
with lifestyles stemming from British institutions.

Quebec is at the heart of the Canadian and North American
francophone diaspora. Its history is filled with unexpected events and
outcomes and numerous contradictions. In the first place, the survival
of the people of French descent in Quebec has contradicted the pre-
dictions of Lord Durham, who in his famous but gloomy report of
1839 on the Quebec situation, shortly after the rebellion of the pa-
triots (1837–9), foresaw the ready assimilation of the French-speaking
Canadians under the pressure of the powerful British institutions.
French Quebec, however, did not raise itself to the high messianic
ideals of the Abbé Lionel Groulx, one of its most impetuous nationalists, who aspired to convince every French-speaking Quebecker and

the French speakers living in the other Canadian provinces of a Catholic and French mission ordained by God (and, therefore, sacred) on American soil. That utopian vision of a French America has maintained itself, as an ideology, among some ultranationalist groups, but gradually lost its appeal when it was confronted by real facts. Today, the francophones' image of North America is that of sheer numbers and of lost territories, not only in the United States and in English Canada, but even in Quebec itself when one pays due attention to linguistic transfers from French to English, as reflected in five-year census data.

From the angle of its cultural reconstruction, Quebec's history is that of the many tensions which existed between the two main ethnic and linguistic communities (the French and the English) aiming at ensuring that their collective rights as ethnic minorities were respected in law and in practice. The francophones, for their part, saw to it that the institutional structures of the central government were respectful of theirs. The anglophones did the same within Quebec's social institutions, particularly at the time of the Parti Québécois government (1976–85). The English–French conflicts have become sharper than ever since the second Liberal government of Robert Bourassa, which followed the election of 1985, has maintained through the use of Law 178, in contradiction to the ruling of the Supreme Court, unilingual French signs outside commercial establishments. As a reaction to the decision of the Quebec Legislative Assembly, the anglophones of the Montreal region established a new political party, the Equality party, and have been successful in having four of their members elected during the political campaign of the fall of 1989. Moreover, the death of the Meech Lake Accord recognizing the distinctive character of the Quebec society, was in a large measure, the indirect, if not the direct result, of Quebec's unwillingness to abide by the ruling of the Supreme Court. The establishment of the Mixed Legislative Commission on the political future of Quebec in the fall of 1990 created a new sociopolitical contest whose definitive outcome is yet unknown for Canada's future as a federal country. So far, one outstanding established fact comes out of the study of the preliminary briefs submitted to the commission (500, we are being told). It is that the status quo ante is being unanimously rejected as an acceptable solution, even by people and groups identified with the federalist ideology. In general, it is felt, that, with the rejection by the rest of Canada of Quebec's basic prerequisites to reintegrate Confederation, Quebec must firmly express a political stance, such as complete sovereignty, in order to impose a type of negotiation with the rest of Canada in which Quebec will be in a position of power, in contrast to the negotiating processes of the past.

The pressure for holding a referendum on the question of Quebec's political status, which was to be held in 1992, is another trend that testifies to the seriousness of Quebec's intentions. Members of the English-speaking community, who have been in Quebec for generations, are prepared to abide by whatever political choice the majority of Quebeckers will make. The Equality party has already committed itself to conform to the views of the majority. I do not know as yet to what extent such stands are being influenced by recent sample surveys where two-thirds of Quebec residents are fully prepared to endorse the idea of full political sovereignty for the Province of Quebec. Contrary to what happened in 1980, the business community is not any longer unwilling to accept full political autonomy for Quebec, if the economic ties with the rest of Canada are retained. To be sure, this is a new political climate that occurs in an unpredictable social environment. There are still unknown factors that may emerge and transform a situation which is so far in line with Quebec's traditional aspirations. What lessons could be learned from the past?

Quebec, a society with a majority of French-speaking residents, has undergone many crises sparked by its bicultural and multi-ethnic composition and by the divergent views expressed within each of the existing ethnic groups regarding their future in a modern Quebec. Land claims and the appearance of a self-determination process among the indigenous peoples (Tremblay 1989) – the aboriginal crisis of the summer of 1990 in Quebec is but a pale reflection of those native aspirations – as well as the ethnic and religious aspirations of some ethnic groups within the educational system in the workplace, and within the information media, are clear-cut, overt expressions of internal frictions. Furthermore, the dualistic ideological split of the francophones, which became manifest at the time of the 1980 referendum, might yet be, up to a point, operational. If, in the past, unanimity was spontaneously established on the basis of survival, today the notions of fundamental ethnic claims and aspirations, of economic development, and of ethnic progress, the main components of a modern Quebec society, *un projet de société*, are being translated in divergent views.

The main elements on which those divergences rest among francophones are several. I shall restrict myself to mentioning the most important ones: the nationalist discourse, which has evolved from a conservative ideology to an ideology of progress and development; legislative reforms that converted the Quebec state into a powerful economic and social instrument of intervention in public affairs and made it the main lever of group promotion, hence the emergence of a nation-state; the new functions and roles of unions and semi-public organizations in the definition of their main fields of competence and of their relationships with government; and individual and collective reactions to cross-cultural relationships, in general, and to the increased and massive influence of the Anglo-American mass media in particular.

It should not be forgotten that the Province of Quebec remained a rural and agricultural country until the Second World War by standing aside in a well-protected cultural niche. The then-dominant ideology justified that closing off by invoking the necessity for the francophones to save their religious, linguistic, and family traditions. That main cultural orientation, principally spelled out by the religious elites that kept a solid grip on the bourgeoisie and the lower classes, was to maintain French Quebec in a state of inferiority in the scientific, industrial, and commercial domains for a long time. The urbanization and industrialization of Quebec progressed at such a fast tempo during the Second World War that the *Belle Province* at that time fully integrated itself into the North American economic and sociopolitical universe. It is to be noticed, however, that values did not change at the same pace as did industrial and commercial structures. This established fact is not much of a surprise to those who are familiar with the ethnological paradigm of change. The astute Maurice Duplessis knew it, and he did not fail to take advantage of such a universal law upon coming back to power in 1944. During the fifteen years that his political hegemony lasted (1944–59), he advocated a return to traditional institutional structures and values, which, in his view, had been profaned by technological changes, the coming into people's attitudes of universal values, and, most of all, by the entry of women into the workforce.

An ideology of catching up was to sustain the strivings of the 'Quiet Revolution' of Jean Lesage (1960–6) and of governments that followed. The guiding principles of that planned transformation were established in reaction to a conservative ideology and did produce a rejuvenation of the state apparatus and did install main social reforms in the fields of education (the democratization of the educational system), of social affairs (the socialization of medicine and the medicalization of social services), and of natural resources (the nationalization of hydro-electricity and other natural resources). These guiding ideals and those socializing practices were to be implemented on a prospective time horizon where the Province of Quebec, while stressing the importance of the exemplary patrimonial value of traditional institutions, would acquire greater autonomy in the management of public affairs relative to the federal state and would make itself noticed for the high quality of its technical and cultural achievements. The hydroelectric development of James Bay and the agreements, then considered exemplary, with the aboriginal peoples, the World's Fair of 1967 in Montreal, the 1976 Olympics in the same city, the International Flower Exhibit, the coming to Quebec City of the great sailing vessels in 1984, the recognition by UNESCO of Quebec City as a World Heritage Site, and some others of a similar importance, all belong to the kinds of achievements associated with the new international personality of Quebec.

The election of 15 November 1976 represents another historical event of great importance for French-speaking Quebeckers. The Parti Québécois, upon taking over the control of government institutions, from the Liberals, put forth new political orientations and challenging development projects. The 1981–2 economic crisis, to which I referred earlier, cast a devastating shadow on that political panorama so filled with high promises, brought about a sudden dismay among the young who had been particularly vulnerable to relatively high unemployment rates, and tarnished the image of the Parti Québécois. It was during that time that the identity crisis of the francophones in Quebec was exacerbated by a crisis of cultural objectives. Quebec then felt the need to redefine itself and take into account its multiple component parts. This occurred at the very time when a closer and more intensive integration into the North America space was taking place with the ratifying, by the Canadian government, in 1988, of a general free trade agreement with the United States.

The Quebec of the 1980s

Since it is out of the question that in this chapter I reconstruct the cultural models and behavioural patterns of traditional Quebec, let me attempt to describe what they have become in the past decade.

The survival ideology, centred on the past achievements of ancestors, is being replaced by a development ideology centred on aspirations oriented to the future. The comparative horizon has become

English Canada. The objectives are crystal clear. The francophones of Quebec have to acquire and master the required expertise in order to get the most important management functions within Quebec institutions. They must build the basic instruments of their economic development and of their social advancement in order to match the level of success of the wealthiest Canadian province, that is, Ontario. A state that has leveraging power (*un état-levier*) is perceived as the most appropriate structure to lead the economic planning and the social development required for such attainments. Quebec wants to build its cultural revolution on modern principles and practices. A third ideological phase, that of national affirmation, coincided with the exercise the political power by a sovereigntist party. The Parti Québécois thus became the main founding factor of an ethnic framework invested with an importance that supersedes all other institutional settings. That party established as its main priority the development of the French culture and installed the kinds of political structures that would gradually lead to a full political autonomy.

Although the general assessment of the Quiet Revolution is relatively positive, the Lesage government did not achieve its main objective, that is, it did not have the leverage to make Ottawa recognize Quebec as a distinct province within the Canadian Confederation. In 1989, the Quebec of Robert Bourassa was again pushed back to the departure line. That lack of recognition became, as we know now, the main obstacle to the successful conclusion of the negotiations between Quebec and Ottawa in order to gain back the rights and prerogatives lost during the Second World War through a centralized process and to ensure the full recognition of privileges rightfully agreed upon by the so-called founding peoples in the British North America Act of 1867. Upon looking back at what happened then, one comes to the conclusion that the state planning carried out by the Lesage government was from top to bottom and failed to rely to a large extent on the needs of the people. Lesage's prospective horizon was too wide and he underestimated the resistance to change. In the extreme, the disenchantments related to unrealistic expectations and the political corruption of the 1950s were the onset of a kind of nationalism oriented towards economic development and political self-determination.

The Breaking Down of the Institutional Frameworks of
Social Cohesiveness and the Cultural Identity Crisis

The rapid social changes which accompanied the transformations of

French Quebec, either in the institutional structures or in behavioural patterns, did not produce only beneficial effects. There exists, at the present time, a questioning of new institutional structures (the privatization of state-owned industries, for instance), conflicting cultural guidelines, and a wide variety of public discourse relating to the content of ethnic identity and to the principles upon which it must rest. Deep discrepancies have emerged between past traditions and those of today. This cultural discontinuity is reflected in the changing patterns of religious beliefs and practices, in the breaking down of the family structure and functions, in the strengthening of materialist values related to a consumer society, in the questioning of the system of authority, in the promotion of individualist values, and in the relative absence of interest toward the voluntary organizations committed to promoting ethnic aspirations. These ruptures, it should be noted, are occurring within the very elements of a civilization that, up to the recent past, had ensured the ethnic viability of Quebec francophones.

One must add to the discontinuities identified those related to the incorporation into the life habits of the majority of an ideology of confrontation that now sets the climate for the day-to-day relationships among interdependent groups, such as those that exist between the state and its civil servants in the public and parapublic sectors, between business owners and workers, between teachers and students, between parents and children, and between men and women. The loss of cultural elements, such as the respect for the civil and religious authority, the submission to those in positions of responsibility, a spiritual worldview, and the quasi-unanimity in value systems, is being accompanied by the acceptance, without any criticism, of a long string of new values. To these transfers in the content of the ethnic profile of French-speaking Quebeckers one must add the continuous pressures coming from the cultural imperialism of the Anglo-Saxon culture. Let me point out some of them: computers and their data bases that reflect alien modes of thinking, pay television that accentuates the penetration of the English-speaking culture, and the mass media in general, all of which make for even greater pressure on the Quebec cultural island. France itself, and other francophone countries, feel threatened by the invasion of the American culture. Thus, it becomes easier to understand why such a small cultural unit as Quebec, a close neighbour to the American Goliath with which it entertains intense commercial, industrial, political, and social relationships, feels so vitally threatened in its foundations and in its legitimacy.

This identity crisis is exacerbated by criticism of the welfare state, and the consequent privatization of state-owned industries and enterprises and shrewd revision of social security measures, and further worsened by the disenchantments regarding the nation-state, a concept which seems to have been discarded following the coming to power in December of 1985 of a party advocating a renewed federalism. Let us refer, first, to the criticisms of the welfare state and, later on, to the defeat of the Parti Québécois government.

In 1985, the Bourassa government won the election by promising to reduce the public debt, to create new jobs for the young, and to re-establish, according to a *bonne-ententiste* ideology, more harmonious relationships with the federal state. It was officially called 'the worthy risk' (*le beau risque*). At the beginning of its mandate, the Liberal government was successful in reducing public expenses and in finding ways to accommodate fluctuating economic cycles by implementing the implicit ideology of the Liberal party, that is, the promotion of private enterprise and of a profitable entrepreneurial state. These economic guidelines were viewed with favour by the public because of the vigour of the North American economy and the lack of alternatives on the part of the opposition party. The Liberals were successful in gaining a second mandate in 1989 despite the election by the Parti Québécois of a new leader, Jacques Parizeau, a prominent ex-minister of the Quebec government.

Let us move now to the disenchantments. One must revert to the economic crisis of the early 1980s. René Lévesque was then head of the Quebec government. As I mentioned earlier, in order to reduce government expenses, his government in 1982 passed legislative measures that were unpopular, especially among those who had re-elected him immediately after the failure of the Quebec referendum, that is, among the young, the new middle classes, the employees of the public and parapublic sectors, people on welfare, and college and university students and their professors. In wanting, in other respects, to regulate the evolution of group identity (*l'identité nationale*) of Quebec francophones through a restrictive view of sociocultural patterns, the Parti Québécois was counterproductive. The use of instruments of economic development, of social promotion, and of ethnic self-development had produced results opposite to those intended. Since the nation-state had gradually become the exclusive symbol of ethnic identity and collective emancipation, it was at the centre of numerous disputes not only among those who shared political succession as an objective, but also among individuals who were willing to consider it. This had negative consequences on the collective self-image of francophones and confused the cultural guidelines that were going to be implemented in their survival strategies.

The failure of the nation-state of the 1980s to yield the expected results could be viewed from another perspective, that of global society. In its governmental functions in a multi-ethnic society, the nation-state had failed to promote the ethnic objectives of those endorsing complete sovereignty for Quebec, in either an exclusive manner or on a general basis without prejudice to non-francophones. It had to manage state affairs in the interest of all citizens, including those who did not share the Parti Québécois ideology. Moreover, the francophone community is itself divided concerning its political future and governmental strategies to be used to achieve due compromises. This ideology is fuzzy about cultural elements to be retained, even, or especially, if linguistic patterns are excluded.

These circumstances in the state made Quebec francophones yet more vulnerable to the invading pressure of Americanism. The ethnic roots of the up-coming generations are very fragile. Difficulties in the labour market and the consequent unemployment of the young mean that *primo vivere* takes precedence over any other worry or goal, including that of the maintenance of their cultural heritage.

CONCLUDING REMARKS

The modernization of Quebec institutions and the pronounced integration of Quebec in the North American sociocultural universe have brought about value conflicts of great magnitude among francophones in Quebec. The crisis of ethnic and traditional values comes up in a new sociopolitical context, that is, one of unsettled trade, of privatization of state-owned industries, and of a revision of linguistic legislation and labour laws. Ethnic values, in particular, are being exemplified in many different models. This is reflected in the collective self-image, in ways of life, and in prospective views, the three social and symbolic universes within which the ethnic future of francophone Quebec is at play.

REFERENCES

Dufour, Christian. 1989. *Le défi québébois*. Montréal: Éditions de l'Hexagone
Gendron, Jean-Denis. 1985. 'Évolution de la conscience linguistique des

CHAPTER 7

Ethnonationalism and Nationalism Strategies: The Case of the Avalogoli in Western Kenya

Judith M. Abwunza

To overcome revolutionary potential in the context of nation-build-ing, often the national self-determination rights of ethnic groups appear to be subsumed in the rhetoric, 'for the betterment of all.' In the case of Kenya, where ethnic groups proliferate, this subsumption takes place through the political production of a national ideology, *nyayoism*, and is enforced by laws against 'tribalism' or 'political ethnicity.' As well, a legitimization of Kenya's one-party form of national government is based on efforts to overcome 'coups and chaos' stemming from 'ethnic alliances and sub-national factions' (Moi 1986: 179). The hegemonic sentiment through edicts for nation-alism and against ethnopolitics in Kenya displays an awareness of the revolutionary potential in the idea of ethnonationalism recog-nized by the government and the people, based on experience during and after colonial rule. This paper investigates the contradiction between government edicts against ethnopolitics and the existence of ethnopolitics as evidenced in the self-determination rights of one ethnic group, along with subsequent self-determination rights of lineage segments within that ethnic group. It also explores how the Kenyan government permits, and may even encourage, this existence of ethnonationalism.

Connor describes as curious that in a world where there is an assumption of a comfortable correspondence between political legit-imacy and ethnic identity within nations, so many nations appear to exist without a principle of ethnic, national self-determination (1973: 1). Recent world events have shown Connor wrong as many ethnic groups within nations are now acting, and more may yet act, for self-determination rights. The sentiment of ethnonationalism does pose a threat to the stability of a nation or at least to the sentiment of nationalism. We note this in past and in present ethnic revolution and foresee it for the future. But it is peculiar that the revolutionary potential contained in significant minority power is not acted upon more than it is (cf. Connor 1973: 1).[1]

In partial answer to this peculiarity, first, it must be said that what is ethnonational in a national context is an empirical question. Second, revolutionary potential is dependent on how national experiences and ideologies correspond with local experiences and ideologies. We may not assume that the creation of a nation, or the revolutionary attempt to create a nation, serves the self-determination interest of all the ethnic groups. We may assume the existence of a presumed, perhaps imposed, hegemonic sentiment which serves to provide a correspondence between political legitimacy and ethnic groups only while the nation exists. We may further assume that this same hegemonic sentiment subsumes the revolutionary potential contained within ethnic groups – only until a revolution happens. The interesting aspect for research is empirical. It involves investigation on both the national and the local levels. Neither one may be dismissed in favour of the other.

The nation of Kenya is a case for consideration. Ethnic groups proliferate in Kenya,[2] and Kenya is included in the long list of countries Connor characterizes as 'currently or recently troubled by internal discord predicated upon ethnic diversity' (1973: 2). Militant events since the summer of 1990 advocating multiparty democracy and the legitimization of these political parties are labelled by many Kenyans as ethnic or interethnic group insurrections. So, worth questioning at the outset is the level of awareness that ethnic groups within a nation may have of their own rights of self-determination. In other words, the rhetoric of self-determination may be articulated nationally in what Connor describes as the nation *idea* (1973: 10), but not ethnically for many people within nations. The rise in consciousness for revolutionary activity (as noted by Marx) within ethnic groups may not be activated. Although the opposite might be assumed, considering past experience, this may be particularly true in cases where colonialism previously existed.

In Kenya, and in other African countries created by colonialism, self-determination underlay the clamour for independence from colonial rule. But in Kenya, *unity* of ethnic groups was a necessary strategy. Once independence was accomplished, it became a further strategy of the new nation's government,[3] to subsume the national self-determination rights of its ethnic groups in the rhetoric, 'for the betterment of all.' The experience of encroachment and unity of ethnic groups against encroachment provided the arena for a hegemonic sentiment that works against revolutionary potential. The sentiment works even more efficiently when a nation provides opportunity for the expression of ethnic self-interest.

THE KENYAN NATION: UNITY, IN *NYAYO* FOR THE BETTERMENT OF ALL KENYANS

The evolution of Kenya's development to independent nation status is well documented.[4] The colonial period produced a country called Kenya to fulfil a British self-interest, a 'white man's colony' at the expense of African humanism, freedom, land, and labour. When this self-interest came under attack by Africans, the British attempted the idea of a 'multiracial partnership.' Partnership with the British translated into control by the British in African minds. Their insistence on independence was to fulfil the self-interest of those Africans considered Kenyans by the British, and by now themselves. One of their demands was universal adult suffrage. This could not be reconciled with any multiracial partnership the British might devise in which Kenyan political representation would be limited to minority power. The British then directed their criticism against African Kenyan independence to what they described as a pattern of 'one-party tribes.' This criticism of political factionalism, along with British opposition to the release and African Kenyan leadership of Jomo Kenyatta, threatened to hold up independence. To counter this, the strategy for independence utilized by some African Kenyan political leaders was to convince African Kenyans that *majimbo*, (Kiwahili: ethnic political unity), would hamper their efforts toward *uhuru*, (Kiswahili, freedom). General political unity would help in gaining it. The Kenyan African National Union (KANU) supported nationalism, and it eventually contained the larger ethnic groups: Kikuyu, Luo, Embu, Meru, Kamba, and Kisii. The Kenyan African Democratic Union (KADU), for the most part, supported regionalism, and it held the allegiance of the pastoralists: Masai, Kalenjin, Giriama, and others. The large ethnic group of Abaluhya was split, but most appeared to support regionalism as they feared Kikuyu and Luo takeover.[5] The result was that the major African political factions eventually joined forces under KANU, with Jomo Kenyatta as the leader of the party and of Kenya. Independence was 'granted' by the imperial power in 1963.

Except for brief periods Kenya has followed a one-party political system with KANU as that political party. Kenyatta (a Kikuyu) remained leader of KANU, and prime minister, then president of Kenya until his death in 1978. Kenyatta was succeeded by the current leader of KANU and president of Kenya, Daniel arap Moi (a Kalenjin). Under both presidents, the dedication has remained to build a 'plural society and multiracial nation,' via national solidarity and sociocultural integration. 'Won by solidarity, our independence demands cementing in solidarity ... For the emergence and survival of a nation, national solidarity is a sine qua non' (Moi 1986: 90). The hegemonic sentiment expressed in political discourse surrounding this was *harambee* under Kenyatta, a Swahili word, usually said to mean working together. Today, under Moi, it is *nyayo*, another Swahili word, meaning footsteps of ancestors. According to Moi, the 'job' of Kenyans is nation-building (1986: 5), and 'there are three important factors in the Kenyan style of nation-building: the vehicle, the force and the philosophy. KANU is the vehicle, *nyayo* is the moving spirit or force, and *nyayoism* is the philosophy' (1986: 18).[6]

Moi sees *nyayoism*, connoting love, unity, and peace, along with *harambee*, sharing through African socialism, as 'the cornerstone of nation-building,' in that it 'integrates the people into a common wholeness' (1986: 21). It is his belief that before 'colonial hegemony and territorial balkanisation' the 'various tribes of Kenya were each a nation or a micro-nation' in that singly they contained the characteristics he believes necessary for a nation: 'the continual upgrading and achieving of a sense of commitment to a common goal by a people; the realisation that they share a cause for togetherness, joint action and mutual improvement, and that they are duty-bound to protect one another's interests and to consolidate a mutual solidarity for the achievement of their common goals' (1986: 21). Today, incorporating *nyayo* as the moving spirit into this former way of life permits the idea of a Kenyan nation, described by Moi as, 'a progressively closer integration, developing a common philosophy of life, identifying common principles, emphasising the integrative trans-tribal and inter-racial forces, subscribing to a common National Constitution under one law, one Parliament and one Government' (1986: 21).

KANU, as the vehicle for nation-building, provides the 'solidification of leadership throughout the entire body politic.' Leadership is 'managed and cultivated' through the process of a national focus, the 'Nyayo focus' (Moi 1986: 81): 'Today, as a continuation and evolution of *Harambee*, *Nyayo* gives Kenyans a stable focus for the promotion of unity, and ... gives unity of leadership management that procreates national dynamism for progress' (Moi 1986: 89). In defence of the one-party system, KANU through a *nyayo* leadership focus 'eliminates the political Babel of tongues within a nation ... leadership focus procreates national solidarity through socio-cultural integration' (Moi 1986: 89–90).

Education for national solidarity, the 'insurance' against subversion, takes place through political guidance and leadership as the president and politicians, 'sparing no energy' travel the country. Moi has written: 'Holding regular rallies, seminars, conferences, etc., throughout the nation (year in year out), my aim has been the practical demonstration of the leadership focus, the creative reiteration of the national principles and the elucidation of the guiding philosophy. The immediate purpose of the meeting might have been ... a passing-out parade for the Police or Armed Forces Cadets, the district fund-raising for the 8:4:4:[7] ... But each occasion has offered an opportunity for national education' (Moi 1986: 91).[8]

Leadership is 'responsive' and 'must evolve from the people, by the people and for the people' (Moi 1986: 97): 'The people must see their representatives to be clean and irreproachable, for nothing teaches like unimpeachable life-styles' (Moi 1986: 101). In Kenya 1988 was declared as the 'year of the clean sweep,' when unclean and reproachable leaders would be 'swept from the political scene.' 'Pollution' of leadership and thus the 'living environment,' is recognized by its salience in the experience of other African nations. Symptoms of 'pollution' are thirteen listed characteristics, from 'colonial hangover' to selfishness killing communal spirit, promoting 'in-fighting and perennial squabbles.' Most characteristics contain some contaminative ingredient intimating the destruction of love, unity, peace, and sharing, thus destruction of the nation. For example, number ix says: 'the perennial bane of tribalism, clanism, septism and nepotism leads to the scenario of political chaos, inveterate suspicion, communal unrest, and a lack of national commitment in all segments of the society, down to the village and homestead' (Moi 1986: 100).

Kenya's system of government contains central, provincial, and local administrations. Criticism is levelled against the central government (for the most part by non-Kenyans, Kenyan criticism would be necessarily muted), for retention of provincial commissioners, district commissioners, district officers, and chiefs in provincial administration.[9] The critics say these positions are a holdover from colonial rule when they were utilized as a measure of control over the African population. Moi's, thus the central government's denial of this criticism is multifaceted and contextual. However, generally the defence states that the criticism against provincial and local administrations does not 'critically evaluate and treasure [their] necessity and contribution ... to our national progress' (Moi 1986: 137). For example, Moi says: 'Today, the Provincial Administration is a system, by which the Central Government ensures that its authority and attendant services do, in fact, reach the people, and are accepted and utilised by them, especially in the rural areas' (1986: 140). This is said to assist in nation-building, further defined as, 'the slow but essential process of creating an organic entity out of the different tribes and races so that, by various activities and programmes, by the infusion of a national philosophy and by the promotion of a convergent psychology, the people are given a sense of oneness; they become a community, a nation, with a common interest and broad general goals' (1986: 141).

The 'demonstrable presence of the ubiquitous authority of the protective and dependable Government and leadership' provides for this idea of nationalism. Among other aspects, 'security' helps, and security depends upon the 'gathering of intelligence at the grassroots' (Moi 1986: 141–2). Through a filter-up effect, it is the duty of the provincial administration to collect, report, and analyse this gathered 'intelligence,' and then pass it on to the government (national) security council, Office of the President. A filter-down effect takes place via the provincial commissioner, who should be 'well connected' to ministers and permanent secretaries via the Office of the President, to local authorities, or 'field officers;' the district commissioner, district officer, and chiefs: 'With regard to important policy issues, the Chief Secretary [who is in charge of public policies] filters the decisions to the Provincial Administration, which passes the necessary operational details to the field officers' (Moi 1986: 145). The committees system, some of them ad hoc, some permanent, is utilized for this purpose.

This system of local government has a long history in Kenya. First established by the British, it continues today in different form under African administration.[10] Local authorities, generally municipalities and county councils, are supervised by the district commissioners who are ex officio members of both municipal and county councils. There are other appointed members of county councils, as well as elected councillors. Within their own designations all 'field officers' engage in corresponding functions. A divisional chief, for example, would oversee a division, 'lesser' chiefs a location, assistant chiefs a sub-location. All are answerable in the filter-up, filter-down information processes, via a hierarchial system that begins in a village, through sublocation, location, division, district, and province, ultimately ending at the Office of the President.

Aside from security measures, the system of local authority is mainly discussed in the 'District Focus Strategy' policy of development (cf. Republic of Kenya 1984). The District Development Plan (Republic of Kenya 1984–8) utilizes local government through the service centre strategy designating by population size four levels of centres – urban, rural, market, and local. Within these centres, financial responsibilities are denoted. All municipal councils are 'required' to be responsible for certain spheres, for example, primary education, health services, and water supplies. Town councils are 'required' to, say, undertake provision of water supplies. The aim in view for national development planning is 'self-reliance for their [local government] revenues and services as soon as possible, so that the Central [and Provincial] Administration may be largely advisory' (Moi 1986: 151). Planning of any nature requires municipal and town councils to form planning units (the committees) and integrate their planning functions with those of the central government's Ministry of Finance and Planning (Republic of Kenya 1984–8).

The strategy for development by the government is self-serving, as ultimately the local governments will become totally financially responsible for their own areas, saving the central government these costs. However, as long as financial self-reliance means paying for their own services, with revenues 'overseen' by the central government, the local government autonomy will be curtailed. For now, the rhetoric attached to 'overseen' is a lack of 'trained staff' on the local level. Trained staff refers to those who fulfil the characteristics of the 'Portrait of a *Nyayo* Provincial Administrator' or 'Calibre of councillors' (Moi 1986: 148–9), which call for commitment to the *nyayo* philosophy at the very least and university education at the most. Lack of these trained people permits an import of Kenyans from other areas. These imported personnel will not be members of the local ethnic group. This is another, important strategy of the central government. For all ethnic groups in Kenya there is a province in which most of the group lives (Republic of Kenya 1979).[11] 'Outside' staff, most particularly the 'field officers' in the system of local government, are vigilant in assessing ethnic or antinational mumbling. Thus, they are of help in providing 'security.'

In summation, the hegemonic sentiment of *nyayo* for nation-building and 'the betterment of all Kenyans,' speaks against ethnonationalism. The nation in Kenya is seen by the government as a system of interdependence between the administration and the people. The administration consists of the central government, the provincial administration, and the local authorities at different levels of one Kenyan society. All administrators in this system must be 'steeped in the *nyayo* philosophy' and are required to be members of KANU. All members of the Kenyan society are required to leave ethnic considerations aside and follow the principles of *nyayo*, and they are 'strongly encouraged' to be members of KANU.[12] The one-party system of KANU is believed by the government to be a necessary requirement to correct the costly disruption of 'intertribal' animosities, as well as 'unhealthy' intertribal and regional disparities. According to Moi:

> There was a need for an active supra-tribal system for the promotion of nation-building and constructive nationalism. Nation-building goes through many traumatic experiences. Kenya cannot be expected to be an exception, for even in the late 1970's and early 1980's there still survived the negative tendencies of tribalism which were preventing the consolidation of nation-building. When it was realised how far tribally based socio-economic organisations were distracting attention from nation causes, my Government dissolved them as soon as it could. The nation's constructive nationalism has been guided especially by the *Nyayoist* principles, philosophy and practice under a de jure one-party system (1986: 175–6).

The system is janus faced between control and democracy in that it provides for a centralized, repressive, controlling regime, while at the same time it appears to permit an image of decentralization and participatory democracy. It is in this image we may search for the ideology and expressions of ethnic politics among one Kenyan ethnic group.

THE AVALOGOLI: UNITY IN ETHNONATIONALISM FOR
THE BETTERMENT OF LOGOLI

Today, 200,000 Avalogoli[13] live in Maragoli Division, Kakamega

District, Western Province, Kenya. From colonial times they have been seen as, and to some extent allowed themselves to be seen as, part of a larger cultural and linguistic Bantu group. This group was first known as the Bantu Kavirondo tribe, a label given by colonials. Later, Avalogoli permitted their own inclusion in a Luhya nation. For a time, this indigenous designation served economic and political purposes centred around ownership of land and independence from colonial rule. In present-day Kenya, they are categorized by the Kenya Central Bureau of Statistics as a subtribe in the main-tribe designation of Luhya. The Baluhya are second in population size in Kenya. Kikuyu are first, and Luo are now third (Republic of Kenya 1979).[14] Like many of their Baluhya neighbours the Logoli people are cattle-keeping agriculturalists with a societal structure of segmentary patrilineage, which to a great extent still legitimizes life ways.

During colonial times in Kenya, all indigenous ethnic groups suffered similar inequalities, for example, alienation from their land, conscripted labour reinforced by pass laws, establishment of reserves or locations, and laws against cash-crop production and trade by Africans. Western Kenya Baluhya opposition to these inequalities began through voluntary associations introduced by the missionaries and adapted by Africans to serve political ends. One of the most salient of these organizations, the North Kavirondo Central Association, was formed in 1932 with the help of the apolitical Society of Friends. It was strongest in Maragoli and Bunyore, the most densely populated areas. But eventually it grew until it had membership in almost every location in Western Kenya. By 1938, this Baluhya association was political, issuing protest against compulsory destocking, demanding payment of war gratuities to dependents of Africans killed in World War I, and campaigning for tax exemptions and the lowering of taxes. Soon the protest was extended to missionaries and settlers, accusing them of stealing African lands. The association's gains were few, and its members often faced persecution from the British. Nonetheless it persisted. In 1939 the association changed its name to the Abaluhya Central Association, thereby legitimizing the idea of a Luhya nation by those people known to the British as the Bantu Kavirondo. Individual ethnic groups assimilated to advocate reserve ownership of land by title deed and to protest against soil conservation measures within the locations. These were seen as a ploy for further European takeover of African land. By the 1950s, an even larger group identity, the Kenyan nation, emerged in the fight for Kenyan independence from the British. Eventually the Baluhya Political Union joined with KANU to achieve *uhuru*. Avalogoli sympathies were squarely on the side of freedom from colonial oppression and any further takeover of land. Their support of Kenyatta's leadership was pledged in 1952, when he spoke to thousands at Mbale Market in Maragoli asking them to unite with all other Kenyans in the fight for African freedom. For some time then, in its history, Avalogoli ethnic group identity was subsumed when its main goal was in Kenyan nationalism advocating independence from Britain. An idea of nationalism evolved that stemmed from membership in religious groups, then crossed religious and ethnic lines to a larger group identity of Baluhya, and finally climaxed in a national identity of Kenyans. This is a good example of Weber's notion about opposition generating identity: 'a specific sentiment of solidarity in the face of [an] other group' (Weber 1958: 173).

Today Avalogoli limit Baluhya identity to mainly urban contexts. National identity is contextual as well. Although the idea of national identity in Maragoli is convincing, as is its political slogan of *nyayo*, the expression of ethnicity, as Avalogoli, apart from other Kenyans, is still pronounced. It persists in a social identity we are able to perceive as Avalogoli ideology, and like all ideologies it is perfect for those who hold it and defensible against those who would interfere with it. Their identity stems from a common commitment to ancestry (for discussion of the importance of this idea see Weber 1968; Barth 1969; Isajiw 1975, 1979); their language, Luragoli;[15] and what they characterize as a 'proper' Avalogoli way of life, where 'one's ethnic cognitions results in ethnic self-identity' (see Aboud 1981). In addition, although their ethnicity emerged from the above characteristics, today it has become an important 'objectified principle' (see Comaroff 1987: 313ff). As a result, their ethnic identity assumes a pervasiveness in their everyday life, including their political life (see Patterson 1977: 102ff). This permits their own interests to be aspired to at the level of collective action, in order to provide not necessarily an aspect of equality (cf. Comaroff 1987: 314), but privilege, compared with those around them in the Kenyan nation.

Ethnicity in African situations centres around a collective claim on a group experience, emphasizing the historical underpinnings facilitating group identity that assists in explaining language and cultural attributes. For Avalogoli, this group experience has been written down by non-Avalogoli[16] and Logoli people themselves. According to the Avalogoli sources (cf. Lisingu 1964), 'a long time ago' Logoli ancients came from a country called Asia. From Asia they settled for a time in Misri (Egypt), then travelled the Nile and arrived in Congo.

From Congo, they travelled overland to Uganda, then crossed Lake Victoria from Uganda by 'canoes made from reeds' to today's Kisumu, Kenya. Some forefathers died on the journey (Mwelesa, no date).[17] A strong wind on Lake Victoria is said to have split up the canoes. The result is that some forefathers went 'south' and some went 'north'.[18] However, 'the grandfather of all was the same person, and wherever people went they left behind those who had the same customs and language as the Avalogoli' (Lisingu 1946).[19] The forefathers of Mulogoli, the ancestor of all Logoli people, stayed for some time ('many years') on the shores of Lake Victoria (from about 1250 AD; Barker 1950: 3). The father of Mulogoli, Andimi, moved farther inland, dying in South Nyanza. Mulogoli, tired of fighting with Nandi and the Masai, moved northwest to Seme, then Maseno, and finally to Mwigono (Maragoli Hills) or Evologoli, today's Maragoli. His brother, Anyore, settled nearby, in today's neighbouring division, Bunyore.

The Maragoli settlement by the ancestor Mulogoli, with his wife Kaliyesa, is considered to have taken place around 1700 (Were 1967b: 7–8).[20] In those old days Maragoli was 'known in two steps, east and west.'[21] Today, Maragoli is divided into North, West, and South Maragoli Locations. A further location division, Central, is projected. North and West Maragoli are the traditional east, and South Maragoli, the traditional west. Mulogoli and Kaliyesa had four sons: Musali, Kizungu, Kilima, and M'mavi. These four sons make up the *tsinyumba tzinene*, 'great houses' in the segmentary lineage structure of the people of Logoli. Mulogoli, 'as all fathers do' gave his sons land. Musali moved north, as did Kizungu. Kilima went to the west and the last born, M'mavi 'remained behind,' in the south, *yatigala nalinda misango gia Mulogoli* – caring for his father's land. These sons and their children spread over the land, in defined territorial segments that for the most part remain today. For example, even though it is empirically established that 'people live all over,' the sentiment of territorial ownership of land puts the *inyumba* (house) of Musali and of Kizungu in North Maragoli, Kilima in West, and M'mavi in South. In terms of authority, the north is the home of the first-born son, Musali, the south of the last-born son, M'mavi, two important hierarchical statuses in the segmentary system.

The names of the sons of Mulogoli, their sons, and their sons' sons are now written for historical purposes: 'To show the beginning of Mulogoli [signifying people] in the world' (cf. Mulama, no date;[22] Lisingu 1946). In addition, a further segmentation of twenty-two

(Mulama) or twenty-five (Lisingu) 'little house,' that is, other grand-
sons of Mulogoli, are also named but not designated into specific
territorial segments. They live 'just anywhere' within the territories of
the four sons. Those who trace their relationship from the four sons
identify themselves in this manner. Some would say, 'we are *avana
va Musali* [children of Musali] here.' This signifies their relationship
to the important first-born son of Mulogoli and permits them to
locate themselves in North Maragoli. In South Maragoli, people say,
'we are all children of M'mavi here,' or, 'we are all children of Mahagira here,' in a sublocation of South Maragoli. Mahagira was the
third-born son of Gonda who was the third-born son of M'mavi, the
last-born son of Mulogoli. Both aspects – territorial segments, along
with birth order from the ancestors – have significance in ethnic
politics.

   Logoli people speak of politics as 'war' and imposition of political
authority as 'being ruled.' For example, they say, 'politics is the same
as war in ancient times, it decides who owns the land and who leads
the people.' Generally they see elections and the elected officials as
corrupt, all 'know' this. Elections can be 'fixed,' for example, interference with those who are standing for election, miscounts, or losing
ballots after the voting process is over. They expect that elected
officials 'will grow fat' in a literal and symbolic sense. All politicians
gain in an economic sense, evidenced by farms, businesses, and
material possessions, and they should also have a 'big stomach,'
symbolic of eating well. The benefit for the electorate is privilege:
Once elected, 'he will remember those who supported him.' Remem-
brance is more astute when the elected official is 'one of our own.'

   Avalogoli political awareness on the national level is informed and
insightful. For the most part their discussion centres on the Kenyan
president. President Moi is seen as benevolent and close to the
people. As a member of the Kalenjin group he provides protection
for the Baluhya against Kikuyu or Luo takeover. He also provides
privilege. For example, Avalogoli say, 'the president is no longer far
away from us,' a criticism that was applied to Kenyatta, a Kikuyu:[23]
'He visits; he assists us; he contributes to our *harambees*.' Interesting-
ly, their experience of presidential closeness is in harmony with the
statements made by Moi above, concerning travelling the country.
However, harmony dissolves in the face of different interpretations.
Avalogoli see that he provides protection against corrupt 'rulers,'
particularly Kikuyu and Luo politicians. It is Moi they perceive as
slapping the hands of other officials, as he says, 'we must do more

for the people.' For example, Moi publicly advocates providing the Kenyan people with government services, helping them to educate their children, or lowering the price of beef. Moi's visits to any area are welcomed with joy. In the Maragoli context people view his visits as providing him the opportunity to recognize their plight and their need for help. They describe the statements made by the President as his attempts to 'clean up' the country. Moi's announcements are given national media coverage and are a topic of discussion all over Kenya. In Maragoli, people say, 'The President has said,' going on to give their rendition, and so his words circulate. A 'probe committee' was set up in the late summer of 1990 under the direction of the Vice-President, in an effort, the people say, to 'let the country breathe' after the 'Kikuyu uprisings' in Central Province. In Western Province, an elder Baluhya woman attacked the visiting politicians on the probe committee, saying, 'You are all crooks, all politicians are crooks, only the President is an honest man' (October 1990). On the other side of the dissolve of harmony, Moi's interpretation of his visits is in the light of 'sparing no energy' to provide political guidance for national solidarity and against subversion.

On the local level Avalogoli political awareness centres on their own member of parliament, the district officer, chiefs, and assistant chiefs with their *magutu* (headmen), Kenyan police (including the Criminal Investigation Department, CID), and members of the local council. The elected MP was known as a 'right hand of the president,' thus, area progress, most particularly improvement to the infrastructure, is credited to his connection and remembering his people: 'He is thinking of us.' The district officer (DO) is an appointed *ummenya* (outsider, non-Logoli). The present DO is a Kikuyu, who 'has been here for five minutes[24] and does not know us.' The chiefs and assistant chiefs have patronage appointments and are Avalogoli, 'ruling' in their own territorial and kin areas.[25] Their appointment is dependent upon their loyalty to the central government. Chiefs are the officials with whom the people have the most contact. Any difficulties are taken first to one's own chief. He makes the decision if problems are to be solved at the local level or taken elsewhere. According to Avalogoli, chiefs 'know their own people' and ought to 'work for their own people.' Government edicts pass down the hierarchy to the chief level and then on to the people through his *barazzas* or visits to their yards. On occasion, a chief's rule is seen to be autocratic and even violent by the people. Chiefs appoint their own *magutu*, who are also territorial and kin based. The *magutu* are unpaid, relying on status perks. Police are recruited and hired and are a mix of Avalogoli and outsiders. Elected council members are Avalogoli, usually overseeing their own territorial and kin area.

The population is captive to the central government. The system on the local level contains the 'field officers' mentioned above, whose loyalty to KANU and *nyayo* ought to be a first priority. The *magutu* patrol their areas during late night and early morning hours and report any findings to the assistant chief, who will send or take a report to the chief. The chief reports to the senior chief of Maragoli, who reports to the district officer. Any serious night-time occurrence or infraction can be reported to the police or 'even to Nairobi' and acted on within hours. However, empirical investigation shows that the state's influence on distinct social segments is highly variable. It is contextual which occurrences or infractions may get reported or how far the reports may go. A report may be stopped at any one of the above levels by kin relations or by the payment of *chai* (tea – euphemism for bribe).

In political discussion, most particularly surrounding nationalism, Avalogoli provide examples of their openness to 'rule' by outsiders. This is usually dispensed in defence of any criticism against 'regionalism' or 'tribalism' (ethnic politics). They are aware of Kenyan laws. The definition of *avamenya* (outsiders) takes two forms depending on context. The first refers to those who are not Logoli people. The second refers to those who are not members of a 'prominent *inyumba*' (PI), that is, who cannot trace descent from one of the four sons of Mulogoli. For example, in the contexts of Maragoli and of South Maragoli leadership, the outsider situation is described as follows:

> To begin with and in the beginning, the leadership of Maragoli people was an *ummenya*, not Umulogoli. The leadership came from Bawanga,[26] to Maragoli. Leadership [in South Maragoli] by [an] Umulogoli came in the 1930's with Agoi.[27] In our sub-location the first person who ruled was not a person of our house. It was an *ummenya* who ruled. And the person who gave [him] the rule was Chief ..., a person of our house. After, [time] this person lost our leadership and [a person] of our house ruled. From him, a person of Musali [first-born son of Mulogoli] ruled. And we lived in peace with these outsiders. These *avamenya* houses during that time we lived with them well.[28]

Those *avamenya* who live in some PI areas in South Maragoli appear to be more numerous than those in other Maragoli areas.

People in one sublocation say their *guga* (grandfather, son of the PI founder) was a 'person of sympathy': 'He was sympathetic to other [little] houses without land from the great grandfather [Mulogoli].' But through the years the PI people experienced and experience that *avamenya* 'rule' is not in their best interest: 'But because in these times [today] when they themselves have chosen to isolate from our house then we have come to be aware, we ourselves have come to know that this is our land. We must have strength and power for all the work and lead it ourselves.' These statements establish the history of the expression of self-determination that is salient among the Logoli people today.

The first government of independence in 1963 installed a son of M'mavi as Maragoli MP in what was called Vihiga Constituency. This was seen as it should be in South Maragoli. This area of M'mavi sons had the highest population in Maragoli. M'mavi, the last-born son of the ancestor had received his father's land. South Maragoli is where the ancestor, thus leader of all Avalogoli, lived. Those in other Maragoli areas 'argued a bit.' Still, this leader, Otiende, was also involved with Kenyatta. He was arrested for his Kenyatta connection during the Mau Mau emergency. Avalogoli say he received his political position by virtue of that connection. However, during his five years in office, Otiende 'forgot the people.' They believe they did not receive privilege.

In 1969, Peter Kibisu defeated Otiende in the general election and took over as MP. In the sense of ethnic politics, Kibisu was an interesting choice for Logoli people. He was *ummenya*, a Muyore, that is he was a son of Anyore, Mulogoli's brother who had settled in the area next to Maragoli, today's Bunyore Division. As further evidence of their acceptance of outsiders as 'rulers,' Kibisu is held as an example. Kibisu's kin group had a war in Bunyore. They 'killed each other in Bunyore and then they left and came to live in this area' (South Maragoli). Also, Kibisu held an important position in the Kenya Federation of Labour, and it was felt that his connection might provide Logoli people with privilege. By this time and, today, privilege is exhibited by 'planning and progress' (development) in Maragoli. However, Kibisu, under direction from the Kenyan government, began to work at 'dissolving the negative tendencies of tribalism.'[29] The Logoli people saw this as Kibisu beginning a political campaign to *kogotisa* (lose) the houses of PIs:

He wanted to lose the names by changing them. For example, we used to call this area [PI]. He didn't want to hear [the name] mentioned. It must just be named [today's place name]. The names were to be only village names, not of kin groups. He refused to accept PI names of places. He rejected all the groupings of all areas in the kinship sense. He rejected all the areas that had major houses. He did this in all areas of Maragoli, when he had power. He understood that if PI names were to be used for sublocations, *avamenya* will not have political power. So this political organization of his did ruin the understanding of the people [confused the people].

Consequently, in the 1979 elections, the Logoli people once more elected a person as MP who they considered to be one of their own, Moses Mudavadi. Mudavadi, who had run second to Kibisu in the 1974 elections, was from the *inyumba* of Musali, that is, the house of the oldest son of the ancestor Mulogoli. During the course of his tenure as MP most Logoli people saw Mudavadi as 'planning for the people ... thinking for us.' His initial legitimacy was acknowledged on the grounds of ethnicity. However, during his time as MP he established himself as a person well connected to Moi, allowing for Avalogoli privilege. He was a branch chairman ('boss') of KANU, the Minister of Local Government, considered by some as the spokesman for the district if not the province, and a close friend of President Moi (cf. *Weekly Review*, 9 October 1987). Moi and Mudavadi were 'together' in the Ministry of Education in earlier days and also had a relationship by marriage, allowing Avalogoli to call Moi 'relative.' At times Mudavadi's tenure as MP was rocky and he was often charged by other politicians in Western Province with wrongdoing. One of his critics was suspended from KANU for a time. On occasion MPs from other areas accused him of undermining democracy by using imagined security reasons to deny MPs opposed to his platform the licences to organize political rallies and fund-raising meetings in their constituencies. He survived the accusations. Most Avalogoli see Mudavadi as a man dedicated to serving them, for example, helping dozens of people get jobs, paying school fees, improving educational standards and facilities, introducing tea growing and a tea depot, and generally developing the area infrastructure, including roads, electricity, a central water source, and markets. Certainly, all this constitutes privilege.

Of further interest for ethnic politics is that not all Logoli people believed Mudavadi should 'rule.' His major contender in the 1979 and 1983 elections was Bahati Semo. People say Semo, is not 'liked, but he is a son of M'mavi,' providing him with legitimacy of rule in South Maragoli. The belief is privilege may weaken if 'one of our own' does not rule. The two, Mudavadi and Semo, are described as having 'deep political differences' (cf. *Weekly Review*, 9 October 1987). Some Logoli people depict them as 'enemies.' At one point Mudavadi became very ill and had to be taken overseas for treatment. The general consensus by people supporting Mudavadi was that he had been poisoned or made ill by witchcraft by people supporting Semo. Mudavadi survived, further adding to his political legitimacy, as a myth of survival grew up around him. By 1986, the two politicians found it necessary to declare a public reconciliation of differences 'for the betterment of the district and ultimately the nation' (*Weekly Review*, 9 October 1987).

In 1986, the Boundary Commission made several changes in Kakamega constituencies, increasing them from eight to eleven. One of these changes involved splitting Vihiga Constituency into two, Sabatia and Vihiga. Sabatia Constituency is made up of North and West Maragoli Locations. Vihiga Constituency takes in South Maragoli Location. In the 1988 elections, Mudavadi, a 'grandson of Musali,' was re-elected, unopposed in Sabatia, the 'land of Musali.' Semo, a 'grandson of M'mavi', was elected in Vihiga, the 'land of M'mavi.' Moses Mudavadi died in February 1989, leaving the people wondering if 'progress' would come to a halt, as his death detached the tie of privilege: 'We do not know what is likely to happen to us now, everything [progress] may end. We do not know who can even take his place.' In April 1989, Mudavadi's 29-year-old son took his place as MP. The obvious candidates for whom ethnic politics is not an issue, for example, any of the nine former political rivals or even the past incumbent, Kibisu, withdrew their candidacy. They are all contextual *avamenya*. Mudavadi's son, an untried politician, was declared MP by President Moi.

Self-determination rights of lineage segments in Maragoli are also in evidence within sublocations, as insider–outsider is played out at the level of chief nominations and council elections. As fathers give land to sons, sublocations are territories of sons of sons in the segmentary lineage structure. Before and during the 1988 elections, many people believed that an endeavour the MP was undertaking was to provide 'old house' leadership in all areas of Maragoli: 'He is putting in *inyumba* people,' signifying people who trace relationship to the four sons of Mulogoli in the hierarchy of birth order. One assistant chief believed his position to be threatened. He was a member of the PI; however, he traced his ancestry to a 'younger *inyumba*,' the third-born son. People in his area were 'heavily' from the 'oldest *inyumba*,' the first-born son. His letters asking the MP for support, along with his own support for a PI council candidate, served him in good stead. He was given a promotion to a chief position.

In one sublocation evidence of this endeavour for 'old house' leadership was provided for the people. The MP declared an 'old house' PI individual the winner of the council seat on nomination day. He instructed people to line up behind the 'chosen' individual and not support the opposing candidate.

The private, political rhetoric for this 'old house leadership' on the local level was 'a movement from darkness to light.' Members of the four founding lineage segments were said by people to be better qualified, that is, more experienced, in leadership: 'It's in their blood.' The central government's public, political rhetoric was the same. However, in its interpretation, it was to encourage all Kenyans to elect educated leaders, who were better qualified by virtue of their education to lead people in a 'movement from darkness to light.'

In most sublocations in Maragoli, it was not all that difficult to find candidates from 'old houses' who were more educated than those from *avamenya* houses. For example, in one sublocation the incumbent for council was an *ummenya* who 'grew here' but was not a member of the PI. When it came time for the 1988 election nominations, a young man with no political experience was chosen to run against this incumbent who had held the council position for two terms. The incumbent has virtually no education (speaks little English, and council proceedings are in English) and is barely literate. The young contender has form IV education. He is also a member of the PI of the sublocation. The theme of his campaign was 'from darkness to light.'

Members of the PI provided the 'real' reasons for their 'fight' against the incumbent. During this incumbent's term in council 'he forgot PI people': 'After the last election he put his own people in [jobs], no PI people.' People's privilege was not maintained. This incumbent's council leadership is also provided as a further example of the danger in permitting *avamenya* 'rule.' The statement 'grew here' refers to his family living in the area for several generations: 'He even claimed to be PI.' A prominent local businessman who suggested the incumbent's initial nomination for the council seat to the MP, and then supported the incumbent in the previous election, changed his allegiance to the young PI contender. He provided the following information in reference to his previous support and then withdrawal of that support; his statements are a defence of ethnic politics: '*Avamenya* would be welcomed by PI people, if they did not try and [sic] take over and run things. He bought votes, but now he is almost out of money, selling [his] land. PI people were stupid allowing themselves to be bought for 5 or 10 shillings. I followed behind him, we shared the same knife [circumcision]. I followed after [sic] him in line ... But he misused his power, taking money for nothing [not following through with promises made for bribes].' The incumbent for the council seat managed to hold on in the nomination process but lost out during the secret ballot election. The PI member is now the holder of the council seat.

CONCLUSION

The peculiarity surrounding the limited revolutionary potential in significant minority power has been examined in the Kenyan nation. Empirical investigation permits our awareness of one ethnic group's expressions and ideology in ethnonationalism. The revolutionary potential in Avalogoli ethnic self-determination is not acted upon even as they experience life under a repressive national regime. Although this is a matter of some peculiarity for outsiders, Avalogoli are not confused by the political complications and contradictions that exist in Kenya. They fully understand where and to whom their responsibilities lie.

National experiences and ideologies have a correspondence with local experiences and ideologies. Avalogoli acknowledge the hegemony of *nyayo* and express it by spoken loyalty to the government along with active participation in self-help through *harambee*. Avalogoli 'right to rule' is produced by their history. In that light, they collectively transform *nyayo*, 'following the footsteps of ancestors of all Kenyans,' into following the footsteps of Logoli ancestors. This allows a pervasiveness of ethnicity in their political life. The pervasiveness permits Avalogoli self-interest in a collective action and provides them with privilege. Privilege may be exhibited in political presence at *harambee* to develop their own area or in occasional government financial assistance. Avalogoli do not view this pervasiveness of ethnicity to be contravening the national principles of *nyayo*. They encounter Moi's and other government officials' visits and contributions to Logoli *harambees*. In addition, from December 1980, Logoli people have participated in a yearly cultural festival, 'the first in the nation,' that advertises their history by artefact and word. Government officials attend these events promoting ethnicity. On one occasion, Moi presided. The Logoli people treat this as evidence of the President's understanding of their ethnicity and his practising of 'grass-roots politics.'

The Avalogoli level of awareness (or rise in consciousness) of their own self-determination rights is so far satisfied by national strategies that overcome any revolutionary potential. National government strategies permit and likely encourage ethnonationalism, even as it contradicts the sentiment of hegemony, 'for the betterment of all Kenyans.'

Government strategy curtails political subversion at the same time as people are provided with the opportunity of democratic process in electing their own political leaders. The system of local government only allows for the inclusion of 'one's own' as political leaders as long as these leaders 'fit' *nyayo* requirements and provide 'first loyalty' to the national party. The subversive element is further curtailed by the watchfulness of the non-ethnic 'field officers,' who must provide the same fit and first loyalty. The Avalogoli transform this fit and first loyalty to their own privilege and to membership in a particular *inyumba*.

Another strategy of the government is to utilize the idea of privilege as a tactic of divide and rule. The government provides enough 'improvements' in Maragoli and within areas of Maragoli to keep the myth of connection, thus, privilege, alive. At the same time it provides 'improvements' in areas outside Maragoli to substantiate that area's own myth of connection, thus, privilege. Enough competition exists among these groups for 'well-connected' leadership of their 'own' and the resulting privilege that a collective action, say, an Avalogoli or a Baluhya political action, is not really seen to be in any group's self-interest. Group privilege against other group privilege is well recognized as it is discussed and acted on by all Avalogoli.

For Avalogoli, collective action in ethnic politics serves their best interests. For the government, thus, the nation permitting some aspect of ethnic politics also serves their best interest. The national hegemonic sentiment of *nyayo* does permit a correspondence between national political legitimacy and this ethnic group. Following contextual 'footsteps' subsumes Avalogoli revolutionary potential, permitting a facade of the supratribal system that Moi sees as necessary to promote nation-building. Avalogoli are able to transform the national hegemony into their own hegemony, through Avalogoli expressions of ethnonationalism. The result is a hierarchical ranking of national allegiance based on privilege: (1) among segmentary structures of Avalogoli; (2) among all Avalogoli; (3) among Baluhya; and (4) 'for the betterment of all Kenyans.' The ultimate strategy of the Kenyan government, most particularly of President Moi, is in producing the national hegemony of *nyayo* that provides opportunity for ethnic groups' self-determination. For the nation, it is likely that a recognition exists that without that tolerance, revolution is conceivable. Even if that self-determination principle is mythological among these politically captive ethnic groups, permitting its ideology and experience halts any revolution. For Avalogoli, a correspondence endures between their ethnicity and national political legitimacy. The Kenyan government tolerates their ethnic ideology and experience of contextual hierarchies of allegiance, while at the same time coercing them into a national allegiance – but only until a revolution happens.

POSTSCRIPT – 1992

A Logoli shopkeeper talks of multi-party politics in Maragoli: 'multi-party is good, FORD, DP and KANU, but KANU should remain the head. The opposition will police the rulers [29 February 1992]. A woman says, FORD is Kikuyu, Luo and some Luhya following Muliro [a Muluhya]. DP is Kikuyu. KANU is still strong here [in Maragoli]. You know Avalogoli, they will decide when they mark the ballot [1 March 1992].'

But a revolution is happening and the media portray the distress with headlines such as: 'Ethnic strife – at least 60 are dead in bloody tribal clashes' (*Weekly Review*, 20 March 1992, p. 3); 'The killing fields: ethnic violence rages' (*Weekly Review*, 1 May 1992, p. 8). In assigning blame: 'The government says it is the opposition. The opposition says it is the government' (Ng'weno 1992).

And to intensify the distress: 'The final split – FORD's leadership crisis breaks up party' (*Weekly Review*, 14 August 1992, cover), into the Odinga (Luo) faction and the Shikuku (Luhya) Matiba (Kikuyu) faction. Masinde Muliro, Luhya vice-president of the splitting FORD, called an 'honest broker' between the two factions and 'a man of principle,' said to be the 'only' compromise candidate as well as the 'leader for the Luhya people' (*Weekly Review*, 21 August 1992), died 14 August 1992.

The historic Kenyan multiparty election was held on 29 December 1992. Moi and KANU were given a mandate in what is described as 'a runaway victory' (*Weekly Review*, 1 January 1993). In Maragoli, Moi and KANU 'remain the head' and the elected sons of sons preserve the right to 'lead the people.'

Acknowledgments

Fieldwork was conducted during 1987 and 1988. Funding for this fieldwork was provided by SSHRC, IDRC, and the Centre for International Studies, University of Toronto. Permission to engage in research was provided by the Department of Anthropology, University of Toronto, and the Office of the President, Kenya. Affiliation was provided by the University of Nairobi and the Institute of African Studies, University of Nairobi. In 1992 fieldwork was funded by a SSHRC Internal Research Grant, University of Western Ontario.

NOTES

1 Leave aside the assumption that the population size of ethnic groups would influence national self-determination. Connor's reference to 'significant minority' (1973: 1) appears to allude to this. Class along with other variables may overrule numbers of people.
2 Kenyan Africans are grouped into thirty-eight ethnic groups, based mainly on ethnic, linguistic, and geographical considerations. Ethnic (called tribal) classification has been restricted to what is designated as 'main tribes' only and 'subtribes' have not been indicated separately, although they were counted as such in the census returns. Forty-one ethnic groups were listed in the 1969 census. The changes affect some of the Kalenjin-speaking groups; Nandi, Kipsigis, Elgeyo, Marakwet, Pokot, Sabaot, Tugen are now grouped as Kalenjin. The Basuba were grouped with the Luo in 1969; today they are recorded as a separate ethnic group, as are the El Molo. Non-African Kenyans are recorded as four groups: Kenya Asians, Kenya Europeans, Kenya Arabs, and Other Kenyans. The non-Kenyan population is recorded into five groups: Africans, Asians, Europeans, Arabs, and Others (Republic of Kenya 1979: 25). Avalogoli, who consider themselves an ethnic group and are so considered by others, are counted in the 'subtribe' classification and included in the larger 'main tribe' classification of Luhya. In some contexts this is acceptable to Avalogoli, in others not (see below).
3 Connor uses the term 'catalytic agent' for more incipient movements. Ethnic nationalism endowed with universal validity becomes: 'The expression [for] the recognition of the remarkable growth in ethnopolit-

ical aspirations, a slogan and spur for movements in progress, and a catalytic agent for more incipient movements' (1973: 10).

4 Bennett (1963) provides a reasonable analysis of aspects of the political history up to Kenya's independence. Gertzel Goldschmidt, and Rothchild (1969) examine the early stages of independence government and nation-building. Gertzel (1970) analyses political aspects of independent Kenya until 1968. Kuria (1991) contemplates the processes of democracy through colonialism to the one-party state.

5 Their political party, the Baluhya Political Union, was one of the most significant ethnic political parties (see below).

6 See Katz (1985) for the development and necessity of *nyayo* discourse. See Abwunza (1990) for the hegemonic status of *nyayo* among the Logoli people and its potential to subsume all possible internal contradictions.

7 The recently adopted system of education.

8 *Nyayo* statements and the president's words are contained in all government documents, in all media presentations, speeches, and general discourse by officials and private citizens. Many copies of the book from which these quotations of Moi have been taken were made available to all primary and secondary schools across the nation. Teachers read and interpreted the passages to the students, the students then passed the information to their parents. The book has interesting internal messages contained within its structure. For example, all chapters are prefaced by 'Quotations From the Author's Speeches.' The preface quote to the chapter entitled 'Intellectuals in Nation-Building,' reads as follows: 'Let me make one thing clear. It is my most positive wish that the whole open atmosphere of freedom in Kenya should be sustained. But we cannot, and will not, tolerate any calculated forces of division or disruption. Anyone setting out to abuse these freedoms we provide is threatening our national integrity, and the defence of such integrity is a duty which, above all else, my Government will always discharge' (Moi 1986: 125).

9 Kenya is segmented into Nairobi and seven provinces: Central, Coast, Eastern, North Eastern, Nyanza, Rift Valley, and Western.

10 Stamp (1986) provides an analysis of the ideology and political practice of Kenyan local government.

11 Central Province, Kikuyu; Coast Province, Mijikenda, Pokomo, Taita, Taveta, Bajun, Swahili/Shiraze, Boni-Sanye, and Orma; Eastern Province, Embu, Meru, Mbere, Kamba, Tharaka, Boran, Gabbra, Sakuye, Gosha, and El Molo; North Eastern Province, Ajuran, Gurreh, Degodia, Somali, and Ogaden; Nyanza Province, Kisii, Kuria, Basuba, and Luo;

Rift Valley Province, Kalenjin, Masai, Nderobo, Njemps, Rendille, and Hawiyah; Western Province, Teso and Luhya.

12 Membership in KANU, as evidenced by one's possession of a card affixed with the required number of stamps, is required to nominate candidates and vote in elections. In addition, 'You will never get a job in Kenya if you are not a member of KANU. If you get into any trouble, no one will assist you if you are not a member of KANU.'

13 In the Luragoli language the morpheme 'Logoli' always occurs with another element. The prefix 'ava-' or 'aba-' yields 'Avalogoli,' the 'people of Logoli' or 'the Logoli people'. 'Mara-' means 'place of ...' Published statistics (Republic of Kenya, Central Bureau of Statistics 2 October 1982) show the Maragoli population as 142,205; however, the census taken in 1987 gives 197,324 as the population count (Provincial Office, Kakamega, private communication).

14 Until 1979, the Luo group was second in population size. The Baluhya have now overtaken the Luo. The Baluhya province of Western Kenya has the highest rate of natural increase in population in Kenya (cf. Ssennyonga 1978).

15 Both English and Swahili are national languages in Kenya. In Maragoli schools the language of instruction is English, and Kiswahili is taught as a language. However, both languages remain very much in the schoolroom or in government offices. Generally, Luragoli is the language of communication. English or Swahili are seen more as languages utilized between Logoli and other groups, rather than among Logoli.

16 Ogot (1967: 72) and Were (1967a: 64–5, 1967b: 7–80 provide historical aspects of the Logoli people. Also, Whiteney (1960), Ochieng (1979), Osogo (1965), and Barker (1950), give histories of the settlement of the area which include the people of Maragoli Division.

17 Mwelesa (no date) has recorded the circumcision sets of Avalogoli, showing the first circumcision in the Maragoli area as 1750.

18 For example, Avalogoli and Avakisii consider themselves brothers. The Kisii people are said to have split off in this manner.

19 This provides the explanation for similarities in language and customs among Abaluhya.

20 Dates are not provided in Logoli sources until the first circumcision in the area of present-day Maragoli; this is recorded as 1750 (Mwelesa, no date).

21 For the Avalogoli, east is life, thus the sunrise; west is sunset and where worship was. The Mung'oma Hills (Maragoli Hills) are considered to be in the west. The caves of the ancients, where Mulogoli

and his people first lived before building houses, are in the Mung'oma Hills.

22 Mulama's Maragoli Map has been printed within the past five years.

23 Being 'far away,' or 'only interested in developing his own people,' was a criticism applied to Kenyatta by Avalogoli.

24 When this statement was made, in 1987, the DO had been in the area for approximately one year.

25 One man described a particular area as 'Chief Mwelesa's kingdom.'

26 This is referring to the installation and imposition of a Wanga paramount chief during colonial times.

27 In the early 1930s the British made concentrated effort to replace imposed chieftainships with local men. Paul Agoi is considered by most Avalogoli to be the first Logoli chief. Mulama (undated) provides a list of the leaders who ruled Maragoli (Maragoli Cultural Map). However, not all Avalogoli agree with Mulama, or even agree among themselves, as to who has 'ruled' in the past.

28 Politics is a sensitive subject in Kenya. Those who inform are therefore given anonymity, hence all the anonymous quotes reported here.

29 See to Moi's quote above, in reference to central government's move against tribalism in the late 1970s and early 1980s. Along with changing names of villages and areas, all organizations that could be determined in any way to be connected with kin groupings or with any ethnic connection were also made illegal. In Maragoli, for example, a number of self-help groups, the Maragoli Association, which for the most part assisted in raising money to return the dead from other areas to Maragoli for burial, football teams, etc. were 'outlawed.' At the same time laws were passed that any gathering of people in groups of ten or more was to be considered 'illegal assembly' unless they were presided over by officials.

REFERENCES

Aboud, Frances E. 1981. 'Ethnic Self-identity,' in R.C. Gardner and R. Kalin (eds.), *A Canadian Social Psychology of Ethnic Relations*. Toronto: Methuen

Abwunza, Judith M. 1990. '*Nyayo*: Cultural Contradictions in Kenya Rural Capitalism.' *Anthropologica* 32(2): 183–203

Barker, Eric. 1950. *A Short History of Nyanza*. Nairobi: East African Literature Bureau

Barth, Fredrik. 1969. *Ethnic Groups and Boundaries*. London: George Allen and Unwin

Bennett, George. 1963. *Kenya: A Political History.* The Colonial Period. London: Oxford University Press

Comaroff, John. 1987. 'Of Totemism and Ethnicity: Consciousness, Practice and the Signs of Inequality.' *Ethnos* 52(3–4): 301–23

Connor, Walker. 1973. 'The Politics of Ethnonationalism.' *Journal of International Affairs* 27(1): 1–21

Gertzel, Cherry. 1970. *The Politics of Independent Kenya, 1963–68.* Nairobi: East African Publishing House

Gertzel, Cherry, Maure Goldschmidt, and Donald Rothchild (eds.). 1969. *Government and Politics in Kenya: A Nation Building Text.* Nairobi: East African Publishing House

Isajiw, Wsevolod W. 1975. 'The Process of Maintenance of Ethnic Identity: The Canadian Context,' in P.M. Migus (ed.), *Sounds Canadian: Languages and Cultures in Multi-Ethnic Society* Toronto: Peter Martin Associates, pp. 129–138

– 1979. *Definitions of Ethnicity.* Toronto: Multicultural History Society of Ontario

Katz, Stephen. 1985. 'The Succession to Power and the Power of Succession: Nyayoism in Kenya.' *Journal of African Studies* 12(3): 155–61

Kenya, Republic of. 1975–80. *Provincial Statistical Abstract, Western Province.* Nairobi: Central Bureau of Statistics, Ministry of Finance and Planning

– 1979. *Population Census*, vol. 2: Analytical Report. Nairobi: Central Bureau of Statistics, Ministry of Finance and Planning

– 1982. *Population Census.* Nairobi: Central Bureau of Statistics

– 1983. *Paths to Rapid Development.* Policy Guidelines on the Department of Social Services. Nairobi: Ministry of Culture and Social Services

– 1984. *District Focus for Rural Development.* Nairobi: Government Printer

– 1984–8. *Development Plan.* Nairobi: Government Printer

Kuria, Gibson Kamau. 1991. 'The Struggle Continues.' *Finance*, 16–31 October, pp. 28–32

Lisingu, Simion J. 1946. *Kitabu Kya Mulogoli Na Vana Veve* (The Mulogoli History and Family). Nairobi: Colonial P. Works

Moi, Daniel T. arap. 1986. *Kenya African Nationalism.* Nyayo Philosophy and Principles. London: Macmillan

Mulama, Don J. (no date). *Maragoli* Cultural Map. Private Publication

Mwelesa, Gideon W.H. (no date). Chart; *Amita Ga Vaguuga Ne Vikevo Via Mulogoli*; *Amina Na Makula Ge Vikevo Via Mulogoli.* Private Publication

Ng'weno, Hilary. 1992. 'Letter from the Editor.' *Weekly Review*, May 1, p. 1

Ochieng, W.R. 1979. *People Round the Lake.* Hampshire: Evans Brothers

Ogot, B.A. 1967. *History of the Southern Luo* I. Nairobi: East African Publishing House

Osogo, John. 1965. *Life In Kenya in the Olden Days: The Baluyia.* Nairobi: Oxford University Press

Patterson, O. 1977. *Ethnic Chauvinism: The Reactionary Impulse.* New York: Stein and Day

Ssennyonga, Joseph W. 1978. 'Maragoli's Exceptional Population Dynamics: A Demographic Portrayal.' University of Nairobi: Institute of African Studies, Paper 8

Stamp, Patricia. 1986. 'Local Government in Kenya: Ideology and Political Practice, 1895–1974.' *African Studies Review* 29(4): 17–42

Wako, D.M. 1985. *The Western Abaluyia and Their Proverbs.* Nairobi: Kenya Literature Bureau

Weber, Max. 1958. *From Max Weber: Essays in Sociology.* Edited and translated by H.H. Gerth and C. Wright Mills. New York: Oxford University Press

– 1968. *Economy and Society,* I. New York: Bedminster

Weekly Review. 1987. 'The Mudavadi Factor.' 9 October, pp. 4–9

– 1992. 20 March, p. 3; 1 May, p. 8; 14 August, Cover; 21 August, Cover

Were, Gideon. 1967a. *A History of the Abaluyia of Western Kenya c 1500–1930.* Nairobi: East African Publishing House

– 1967b. *Western Kenya Historical Texts.* Nairobi: East African Literature Bureau

Whiteney, W.H. 1960. *The Tense System of Gusii.* Uganda: East African Institute of Social Research

 CHAPTER 8

Biafra and Bette: Ethnonationalism and Self-Determination in Nigeria

Michael D. Levin

Nigeria, one of those great federal creations of British imperialism, is usually described as a nation divided into three ethnic groups: the Igbo, the Hausa–Fulani, and the Yoruba. The conception of Nigeria as being composed of three dominant peoples whose relations determine the politics and the peace of the country is the one most commonly known abroad and is also dominant in the Nigerian popular press.

This image of a nation of three 'tribes' is a tribute to the power of administrative structures to create symbols. To reduce a cultural reality of at least 200 groups, linguistic or ethnic, and a population in which minority peoples make up at least forty per cent of the population, to the magic number of three is an achievement not to be underestimated. The Eastern Region was predominantly Igbo, the Western, predominantly Yoruba and the Northern, Hausa–Fulani. The consequences of this 'ethnic reductionism' have been not only opportunities for superior anthropological irony, but have been tragic for Nigeria and for many Nigerians fatal.

The creation of Nigeria, the integrative pressures consequent on creating a civil state, stimulated new forms of ethnic self-awareness. The larger peoples were given de facto constitutional recognition; the smaller peoples, 'the minorities,' were cast into a residual category. Numbers rather than cultural substance mattered. The majority peoples were seen as making politics and history; the minorities were drawn along, struggling to make alliances and find a place in Nigeria balancing ties with the region against ties with the federal centre. The most dramatic event of Nigerian politics, alternatively named the Biafran Secession or the Nigerian Civil War, was a direct result of this tripartite conception of Nigerian cultural divisions and its use as the basis of the Nigerian federation. Remarkably, given the reputation of African states for intergroup tensions, in the two decades since the end of the civil war, Nigerian politics and constitution-making has transformed the state to a point where ethnic politics as such have been accommodated in the political system and although 'sharing the national cake' remains central to politics, ethnicity is being muted in favour of regionalism and representation on the basis of population.

Ethnonational conflict in Nigeria reached its peak in the brief life of the secessionist Republic of Biafra. Biafra was characterized as the expression of Eastern aspirations for self-determination. Independence and the necessity of self-determination for Biafra were identified with survival for the Easterners, who had suffered expropriation, violence, and murder in other regions of Nigeria. The Region having in place the bureaucratic structure, the jurisdictional definition, and a defined territory provided the form of the new state. The Igbo were the majority in the Eastern Region and 'Igbo' and the 'East' were often synonyms, for the uninformed, but the Eastern Region was not exclusively Igbo and members of the many non-Igbo groups suffered and escaped the fate of many Igbo in riots and massacres in Western and Northern cities. The ambiguity of difference in meaning between East and Igbo meant tragedy for some and salvation for others. It was this difference in experience during the crisis leading to secession and the difference in historical experience in the Eastern Region that informed attitudes to Biafra and secession. The Biafran Secession is both a focus of this paper as the expression of Igbo-Eastern ethnonationalism and the context for the story of the Bette, a minority Eastern people, whose political aspirations have not crystallized as ethnonationalism.

The Igbo are the majority population in the former Eastern Nigeria. The Bette, a small ethnic group in the Obudu Local Government Area in the northeastern corner of the former Eastern Region, is one of many such groups south and east of the Igbo. The Igbo experience can be viewed as classic ethnonationalism, its rise and decline in Biafra the expression of the identity between ethnicity and the goal of a nation for a people. The Bette experience before, during, and after the Biafran episode has two defined sides: the response to the Igbo majority and its Igbo-Eastern ethnonationalism and the development of ethnic self-awareness from a minority status.

BIAFRA AND ITS CONSTITUTIONAL ORIGINS

The climax of the Biafran drama was the civil war. The Biafran Secession was also the climax of the conflict between the two constitutional models for Nigeria: the three-regions model and the multi-state model. Without the three-regions model, 'a charter for Regional obscurantism,' the Biafran Secession would not have been possible (Arikpo 1967: 157). The civil war, the Biafran War of Independence, this climax of the Biafran drama, fought not only to preserve the East against the other regions, but ironically also to preserve the big 'tribe' hegemony over smaller peoples has been the most defined episode of ethnonationalism in Nigerian history. But secession was not a goal shared by all Easterners. Secession would have taken the Eastern Region minorities, between 40 and 50 per cent of the population, out of Nigeria into a new state in which they would have been opposed to an Igbo majority.

This polarization between the Igbo and eastern minorities did not begin with the Biafran period. The 1950s movement for a Calabar–Ogoja–Rivers (COR) State, was for a non-Igbo state. Voting patterns in the pre-Independence Regional House of Assembly elections reflected this opposition (Coleman 1958 cited in Nnoli 1980: 172). So, as Igbo desire for self-determination intensified, minority self-awareness was sharpened. Nigerian politics in this three-regions system can be simplified as access to federal power and to the regional centres. In the latter Igbos dominated access, therefore separation from the East but within Nigeria for minorities was a route to greater autonomy and self-determination.

To account for the development of the political situation that precipitated the Biafran secession it is necessary to give a brief history of the development of the Nigerian state in terms of its structure and its relationship to ethnic images. The popular image of Nigeria as a country of three ethnic groups is one dimension of this development, and it is possible to show how it was formed and intensified, indeed made real, by the administrative structure and constitutional framework established during the colonial period ending in 1960. But the colonial period also saw the intensification of self-awareness of many ethnic groups, a process that was also the result of administrative practice and national development.

As Nigeria was being formed it was defined in contrasting terms which were the result of the timing of conquest, the pre-existing forms of trade, and indigenous political structures. Sharp distinctions were made between North and South and then in the South between East and West.[1] These distinctions reflected religious, cultural, and geographical criteria. The boundary was an approximate limit of the southern extension of Muslim influence and the northern extension of 'cultural' affinities of Yoruba and Igbo. It was also an approximation of the watershed between rivers flowing north to the Niger and Benue, or south to the Niger and the sea. (The Niger's source is far to the west of Nigeria in Guinea, and it arcs northeast and then descends southeast through northwestern Nigeria until it turns south to the Atlantic.) This tripartite division formed the basis of the three regions model.

The exigencies of local administration in many parts of the country, but especially where states had not existed in the precolonial era, led to the programs of research into local political organization which in turn generated the conditions for ethnonational aspirations. After the failure of the initial attempts to organize administration from the top down, research by colonial officers in the late 1920s and early 1930s into indigenous politics and culture provided information used in establishing what were called Native Administrations and Courts. The use of indigenous languages engaged peoples in the process of describing their own societies and customs. Names were 'given' to peoples who did not have terms for self-description. The research process helped establish ethnic conceptions and linked them to land. Native law and custom became an important element in British colonial administration (cf. Bohannon and Bohannon 1953; Levin 1990).

By the time the post-World War II constitutional process was fully under way self-awareness of cultural difference extended not just to neighbouring peoples, but to some broad sense of Nigeria. As more and more people, mostly men, had travelled from their villages to other parts of Nigeria and abroad as soldiers and students, concepts of Africa, Nigeria, and Europe took on broader and deeper meanings. 'Tribal unions' were established, especially in towns and cities, for social welfare purposes but also to represent their 'people' in local and national politics. As the awareness of the 'other' expanded and became more definite, the sense of uniqueness in each group intensified (Connor 1973: 4).

The constitutional process attempted to reconcile the complex cultural and linguistic reality of Nigeria with a notion of national unity. Two main models of a national system and constitution competed: a three-regions model with majority ethnic groups as the anchor of each region, and more complex models grouping peoples into four or more regions. These opposed models dated back to the early 1900s when the amalgamation of Northern and Southern Nigeria was being discussed by the British authorities. It was the three-regions model that was chosen then by Lugard, the conqueror and first governor of Northern Nigeria and the first governor-general of amalgamated Nigeria. Lugard's vision of a 'united North' continued to be sustained in subsequent constitutional conferences (Crowder 1978: 196–7). Early in the postwar period during the pre-independence constitutional conferences warnings were already being voiced: 'many young Nigerians were apprehensive of the incipient centrifugal tendencies which had been nursed by the Richards Constitution and of the growing antagonisms which were developing between North and South, Ibo and Yoruba, nationalists and legislators' (Arikpo 1967: 66) In the final nationalist–British constitutional conference in 1954, before Independence, the three-regions model was continued despite minority representations and an inquiry into minority questions, and later in 1960 was adapted as the Constitution of the Republic (Arikpo 1967: 85–103). The NCNC, the political party which aspired to a national constituency but was identified with Eastern and Igbo interests, initially supported a unitary constitution and a federation of small states, in principle minimizing the differences between ethnic groups and, in effect, challenging the hegemony of the large ethnic groups and their regional bases (Crowder 1978: 229). While this policy could be seen as open and universalistic, it could also be interpreted as giving advantage and protection to Igbo migrants in other parts of the country and this perception was a source of resentment and suspicion. The stage was set for inter-ethnic conflict. Igbo and Eastern migration to other parts of the country came under attack and the coup of January 1966 confirmed fears about the extent of Igbo ambitions.

The success of the three-regions system depended on the development of a set of alliances on the national level between the majority group in each region with the minorities in other regions which would, it was predicted, lead to overall balance in the system with no major group wholly dominating minorities of its region. Such alliances were made, but the balance did not last under the pressures of the almost total dominance in each region by one party. Moreover, the triad of regions lead on the national level to a series of two-on-

one coalitions, with the North and one of the southern regions against the other southern region. The language used to describe the situation reflected its volatility: the three-regions system had 'incipient centrifugal tendencies' (Arikpo 1967: 103), because the '3 player ethnic game' (Young 1976: 289) was based on 'big tribe chauvinism' (Sklar 1971: 54). Dominant in their regions, overwhelming in the majority in the regional offices, in the police force, and in urban occupations, the three major groups came to see themselves as the competitors, or rivals, for national state benefits. The three-regions system enhanced their importance at the expense of all other ethnic groups. The idea of all the Igbo people, a new concept, originating in the colonial era, became part of a new question in the era of independence. Which of these three ethnic groups should rule Nigeria? As one writer has put it, ethnic politics was 'incandescent' in the 1960s in Nigeria (Young 1982: 91). The breakdown of order, of electoral politics, and of civilian rule, in Nigeria in the six years between independence in 1960 and the first military coup in 1966 has been well studied. The first coup, the unitary government imposed by the military, the ethnic identification of the coup and counter-coup, and the ethnic riots and massacres led to the civil war.

The precipitating constitutional step to the secession of Biafra was the declaration on 27 May 1967, by the Federal Military Government of twelve states, three of which were in the former Eastern Region. In barely a year, Nigeria had swung from a three-player ethnic game to a unified system with negligible regional representation, in any sense, to a multistate system with a strong federal government. The Eastern Region under Lieutenant-Colonel Odumegwu Ojukwu had no confidence in the federal government and declared within a few days, on 30 May, secession of the region and the new Republic of Biafra. Thus, the East from which there had been advocates of a role for strong central government and small states, was now fighting for the integrity of its region and measuring Nigerian politics in terms of regional interests and opposing small states. The polarization of Nigerian politics into opposition of North against South, Igbo against Yoruba, led to the breakdown of order. A series of coups which were seen as ethnically motivated, massacres of Igbo and other Easterners, the alienation of the East from the Nigerian nation, and the evidence that Igbo lives could not be protected outside the East resulted in the desperate secession of the East motivated by the instinct for survival and the ideal of self-determination.

The Igbo story fits the simpler definitions of ethnonationalism:

ethnic self-awareness and the idea of popular sovereignty, of being a people and legitimizing the desire to be a nation. The elevating of Igbo ethnicity to identity with the Eastern Region and the identification of the other majority ethnic groups with 'their regions,' however, was paralleled by the awareness of the many other ethnic groups in Nigeria of their unique cultures and the alientating fact that in the three-regions system they were politically marginal. For the Bette of Eastern Nigeria, the Biafran secession was perceived as an intensification of this political marginalization.

THE BETTE – MARGINALITY AND ETHNICITY

The position, physical and political, of the Bette is best understood in the context of their geographical and socioeconomic situation. The very description of their circumstances, as apparent to them after forty years of colonial rule as to outsiders, is part of the explanation of their very modest ethnonational expectations.

Bette, the people, number about 30,000 persons and live in sixteen villages in the northeast of the Cross River State. Their northern boundary was with the Northern Region across which are the Tiv, a larger minority people, their 'traditional' enemies. Obudu, a town of about 5,000 persons is the administrative and market centre and the only town in the Obudu Local Government Area (LGA). The Bette are one of six ethnic groups in the Obudu LGA, three of which claim genealogical relationship with each other and with other groups west of Obudu and in different modern jurisdictions. Although they have occasionally been activated in fighting with the Tiv, these traditional political ties are rarely acknowledged in everyday modern politics as territorial continuity and administrative criteria have become more important criteria of solidarity.

The Bette 'clan' was named in 1932 by a colonial officer and for a number of years was a separate Native Authority (Stoddart 1932; Levin 1990). It was only in the 1930s that traditional affiliations came to play an important role in the conception of local government and administration. This administrative unity was based on the colonial philosophy that traditions provided the ideology for solidarity and cooperation. These traditional affiliations were discovered through colonial field research and came to play an increasingly important role in the conception of local government and administration.

The local situation, its boundaries and structure, appeared to be stabilized through the somewhat arbitrary processes of colonial rule, while beyond Bette and Obudu, the jurisdictional envelope moving with Nigerian politics continued to change and was in contrast dynamic. First contact of Bette with Europeans – British military officers – was in 1910. Bette was grouped jurisdictionally in the beginning as part of the Obudu Sub-Division with its ancient enemies, the southern Tiv clans, and other neighbouring peoples, related and unrelated. Obudu Sub-Division had as its northern boundary 7° N latitude, a neat horizontal line on a map, a form of cartographic aesthetic. As cultural and political realities became known to the British administrators this unrealistic boundary grouping together traditional enemies was changed to a line of cultural and political, or ethnic, difference. This boundary was also the line of demarcation between the Southern Protectorate and the Northern Protectorate, and later, in 1914, between the North and the East, when the South was divided into two, East and West. As the national system of Nigeria developed, Obudu, the local jurisdiction, retained its name, but had its status changed and adjusted as it became a division in Ogoja Province, which comprised several such divisions. Since the 1950s boundary adjustments, usually initiated locally, have used ethnic or cultural criteria for inclusion or separation, thus shifting peoples between Obudu and neighbouring divisions.

The colonial state not only created Bette as a people (as it did the Igbo), but defined it as 'a place,' given it a position in the economy and politics of Nigeria. This place is part geography and part politics. The Bette location on the Eastern-Northern boundary has been significant for Bette perspectives on Nigeria and participation in Nigerian life. In the past forty-five years the progressive expansion of the Nigerian state has increased the integration of Bette and Obudu institutions into the national system. The main instruments of this integration have been the expansion and improvement of the road network and the growth of the educational system. Throughout the colonial period Bette had been migrating to work in towns and cities beyond Obudu and the East. This migration reached significant numbers at all levels of the occupational structure after the end of the Second World War. Destinations were not confined to the Eastern Region. As road travel improved communications among Bette in different parts of the country improved.

Education has been the other means to mobility, both spatial and occupational. Obudu Boys Secondary School was built in the 1960s, the Girls' Secondary School shortly thereafter; local co-educational secondary schools in some villages have been built since 1975. Education has been the route of occupational mobility, which for the Bette also means physical mobility to the larger towns and cities.

This intensifying process of integration has since 1946, when the regional structure of Nigeria was established under the Richards Constitution, allowed the Bette to develop a sophisticated understanding of how political structure affects life chances and political benefits. This understanding is not unique to Bette, but the Bette understanding is coloured by their own minority standing. They have developed a broad national perspective; some were attached through educational experience or work with Kaduna in the North, or Lagos, the federal capital in the West; others were associated with Enugu or Port Harcourt in the East, later to be in Biafra. The complexity of Bette political involvement included not only support for the NCNC party, which dominated the East and was identified with the Igbo, and the Action Group, an advocate of minority rights though based in the West, but also for the movement for the COR State, a state composed of the non-Igbo minorities of the Eastern Region. This national orientation with ties to urban areas in many parts of the country was the Bette situation in 1967 as the political crisis came to a head with calls for Eastern secession.

The Federal Military Government's declaration on 27 May 1967, creating twelve states and making Obudu part of the Southeastern State did not make itself felt in the Eastern Region, which three days later seceded as Biafra. What might have been joy for Obudu and Bette was overshadowed by anticipation of war. For the Bette, secession was not welcome news. It divided Obudu people. The two centres of political and business activity, Lagos and Enugu, were now in different nations. The vast arena of Nigeria was now a smaller field of Biafra. The ethnodrama of victimization, of mob and military murders affected them differentially. Bette were not Igbo; they had suffered as Easterners in some places, but had been distinguished from the Igbo in others. In Biafra, Igbo chauvinism competed with Eastern, or Biafran, solidarity. Igbo policemen, Igbo officials, Igbo shopkeepers and traders represented a dominant majority; the Igbo language became a symbol of solidarity that the English-speaking Bette elite had to reject. One schoolteacher in the early tension-ridden days of Biafra, as we walked down the middle of the road after dark, commented that Biafra was not good for Bette, or the people of Obudu – they needed a big country to find opportunities in; not being Igbo was going to make life difficult. He went on to explain that what we might call 'the ambiguity of minority ethnicity' had different advantages in different parts of the country. The politics, or more correctly, the suppression of politics, in a war-threatened Biafra, did not allow any expression of opposition to the centre from the periphery.

But, the experience of living in Biafra was brief for the Obudu peoples, a mere six weeks. The civil war began in early July and within a few days Obudu fell to federal troops. (Although not officially an occupation, this liberation was harsher and more damaging than the secession and the war itself.) Civilian administration was established in liberated areas as the Southeastern State, but routine daily life did not return to normal until the end of the civil war in 1970.

Because of their minority position, Bette politics was per force, despite the intensity of Nigerian ethnic politics universalistic in tone, seeking alliances with others to escape Igbo hegemony. The Southeastern State and the new form of state politics did not end the agitation for more and smaller states, either for Bette or in other parts of the country. In 1975, the name of the state was changed to the Cross River State and divisions became local government areas (LGAs). In 1987, Cross River State was divided into Akwa Ibom and Cross River, leaving Obudu and Bette part of Cross River.

Bette 'separatism' has known two historical moments: its several years as a Native Authority, which became too expensive to maintain apart from other Obudu peoples, and a brief moment of farcical excess during the civilian regime of 1979 to 1983. The Cross River State (and, it must be noted, other Nigerian states) planned to divide their local government areas, multiplying the number by three. Where there had been seventeen LGAs, there would now be fifty-one! The logic employed was irresistible. The financing was virtually nonexistent, and the cultural basis was weak. Bette would have achieved autonomous local government status, despite having no administrative centre and no regular market. Bette villages were planning more divisions of the body politic, by elevating or renaming lineage heads 'chiefs.' Lineage segments that had distinct areas of residence in precolonial days, but now had dispersed and intermingled among each other were planning to declare themselves 'villages.' No one defended the process as anything but cynical, a method of expanding the share of the resources of the state. This kind of political-administrative self-indulgence, which also included abolishing local head taxes, the only tax most Nigerians paid, was brought to an end by a military coup on 31 December 1983.

In both the Igbo and Bette cases we see that it was not the linguistic or cultural dimensions that were uniquely the basis for ethnic awareness, but it was the kind of state and the colonial origin of that state that shaped the ethnonationalism of its peoples (cf. B. Anderson 1983). The Igbo could be drawn together as 'a people'; self-awareness could be developed by deliberate and purposeful politics, and they had a base in the Eastern Region. The Bette to resist domination were forced to elaborate their self-conception as an ethnic group and were compelled to seek alliances to gain recognition for 'minorities'. The cultural side of ethnonational development, the 'natural' conversion of language and culture into jurisdiction tempted Bette only for a brief cynical time. The Bette perspective on ethnonationalism has been a universalistic view on how questions of cultural differences in politics should be dealt with and, it can be argued, because of their small population, it had to be so.

AFTER THE CIVIL WAR

At the end of the civil war in 1970, General Gowon, the Federal Military Governor, declared there should be 'no victor, no vanquished,' and twenty years later his wishful declaration seems to have been achieved. The overwhelming national postwar theme has been reconciliation. Biafra itself disappeared into the multiple state structure of Nigeria.

In most parts of Nigeria, even those where easterners were massacred, Igbos and other easterners have re-established themselves in business and trades. In the Igbo areas multiplication of states has also taken place. The East Central State of 1970 was divided into Anambra and Imo States in 1975. Open and vigorous Igbo participation in Nigerian politics has, however, been somewhat muted. (In 1991, the number of states from the Igbo areas of the former Eastern Region was increased to four.[2]) In the post-Biafra period there was some sense of Igbo reluctance to press issues and federal withholding of funds and other resources from the former Biafrans.

For the non-Igbo states carved out of Biafra, out of the old Eastern Region, however, the issues of Igbo hegemony and the goals of COR State activism are alive in their policies. The non-Igbo areas to the east and south of the Igbo formed two states in 1970, Southeastern and Rivers, and in 1987 three, Cross River, Akwa Ibom, and Rivers. (In 1991 the total number of states from the former Eastern Region was seven.) These states have enacted policies and influenced the federal government to enact policies which limited the Igbo return. Special commissions were created to sell 'abandoned property' and the regional system which benefitted Igbo landlords has now been replaced by the states with one that is being used to benefit indigenous landlords, the purchasers of the 'abandoned property.' Igbo return has been limited to merchants, while public service jobs and land ownership is limited to indigenes.

For the Bette the period from 1970 to 1988 was one of the assertion of local power. The main forms of this were the use of political and ethnic ties to obtain benefit from national and state programs in health and education which were spurred on by oil boom revenues. Funds for village- and clan-sponsored maternity clinics and secondary schools and the locations of national institutions were the main prizes. These issues fuelled a continuation of 'new state' politics and the case for a division of Cross River State. Bette and Obudu became strong supporters of this division. No longer in an ambiguous status, as they were in the three-player ethnic game, the Bette and other Obudu peoples now had much to gain by being in a yet smaller state. The new Cross River State was established in late 1987. The main benefits are likely more political appointments for Obudu and Bette persons.

The major theme of Nigerian history and politics in the three decades since independence, coming to terms with pluralism, reached its climax in the civil war. The brief separation of Biafra, its idealistic expression of popular self-determination, its fragility supported by ingenuity and resourcefulness, make it – at least for some – a romantic moment in Nigerian history. For others it was a tragedy, treasonous and motivated by ethnic chauvinism. The Biafran episode, however, also is an example of the potency of ethnonationalism, how, in only very few years, a decade or two, identity can be formed and the symbolism and sense of being 'a people' created (Young 1983; Coleman 1958). Whatever the view in retrospect the collapse of Biafra did mark the death of the idea that the system of a few big regions anchored by large ethnic groups could provide stable government. The big regions model was replaced with a more flexible one: multiple states in a strong federation came to be the Nigerian form of political development. The multiple-state system also allowed recognition of cultural differences to be accomodated within the political system and separation of legitimate interests from corrupt tribalism (Ekeh 1990). The flexibility of the multistate system, dividing even the very large ethnic groups, the dominant players in the old system, into one or more states, has shifted attention from ethnic issues to economic questions as the criteria of fairness, and weakened the view that ethnicity is the only basis of solidarity and its existence therefore always a threat to national unity.[3] Both Igbo and Bette ethnic identities have been made more secure as the separation between ethnicity and politics has increased.

NOTES

1 The Niger and Benue Rivers divide Nigeria into three parts, and the jurisdictional boundaries roughly imitate this division, but the North–South boundary is to the south of the rivers and their junction.
2 In August 1991 three additional states were created affecting Igbo populations: Anambra was divided into Anambra and Enugu States; Imo into Imo and Abia; and the Ibo populations west of the Niger separated, with others from Bendel State in the Delta State. The campaign beginning in early 1991 for new Igbo states to give Igbo a fairer share of national revenues was noted as a return of the Igbo to full public participation in Nigerian politics, to speaking out as 'Igbos.'
3 In August 1991 the Federal Military Government created nine additional states raising the number from twenty-one to thirty. Seven states had been added to the original twelve in 1975, another two in 1987.

REFERENCES

Anderson, Benedict. 1983. *Imagined Communities: Reflections on the Origin and Spread of Nationalism*. London: Verso
Arikpo, Okoi. 1967. *The Development of Modern Nigeria*. Baltimore: Penguin Books, Penguin African Library
Bohannon, P.J., and Laura Bohannon. 1953. *The Tiv of East Central Nigeria*. Edited by D. Forde. London: International African Institute, Ethnographic Survey of West Africa
Coleman, James S. 1958. *Nigeria: Background to Nationalism*. Los Angeles and Berkeley: University of California Press
Connor, Walker. 1973. 'The Politics of Ethnonationalism.' *Journal of International Affairs* 27(1): 1–21
Crowder, Michael. 1978. *The Story of Nigeria*, 4th ed. London: Faber and Faber
Ekeh, Peter P. 1990. 'Social Anthropology and Two Contrasting Uses of Tribalism in Africa.' *Comparative Studies in Society and History* 32(4): 660–700

Fardon, R. 1987. 'African Ethnogenesis,' in L. Holy, (ed.), *Comparative Anthropology*. Oxford: Basil Blackwell, pp. 168–88

Levin, Michael D. 1990. 'Creating Identity: Colonial Administrators and the Definition and Reorganization of 'Clans' in the Early Colonial Period.' Unpublished paper

Nnoli, Okwudiba. 1980. *Ethnic Politics in Nigeria*. Enugu: Fourth Dimension Publishers

Obasanjo, Olusegun. 1987. *Nzeogwu*. Ibadan: Spectrum Books

Sklar, Richard. 1971. *Nigerian Politics in Perspective*. East Lansing: Michigan State University Press

Stoddart, A.F.R. 1932. *Intelligence Report on the Bendi–Bette Clan, Obudu District, Ogoja Province*. Enugu: National Archives, EP 8880 CSE 1/85/4674

Young, Crawford. 1976. *The Politics of Cultural Pluralism*. Madison: University of Wisconsin Press

– 1982. 'Patterns of Social Conflict: State, Class, and Ethnicity.' *Daedalus* 111(2): 71–98

 CHAPTER 9

Ethnicity and Aboriginality: Conclusions

Michael D. Levin

It is clear from these papers that ethnonationalism is not a unitary phenomenon despite similarities in the language and the form of conflicts it engenders. Two common views of ethnonational politics as either very simple (special pleading concerned only with parochial interests) or complex (with an overwhleming number of clamouring groups each seeking advantage) are both caricatures of the issues. The cases in the present collection fall into neither extreme, but illustrate certain features of ethnonationalism that have depth and complexity. The language of ethnonationalism, for example, places the ethnic group within the state and variously structures the debate in different countries. Another main area of discussion is the role of the state itself in issues of ethnicity and its politics. All the papers in the collection deal with these two themes in some way. It is useful to keep these topics separate, although the state, and its culture, powers, and rights so dominates the issues that it becomes the centre of discussion and engulfs other topics. The language of ethnonational politics has a separate evolution as ethnonational claims come to be recognized and gain increasing legitimacy.

THE LANGUAGE OF ETHNONATIONALISM

A major step in recognizing the legitimacy of ethnonational politics is accepting, as do the papers in this collection, that the stigma of ethnicity has been replaced by recognition of its universality (Glazer and Moynihan 1975). The view of ethnic groups as minorities, which often carried the sense of numerical and moral inferiority, has been replaced with confident assertions about self-determination. Claims which were once voiced as pleas for understanding and compassion are now made on the basis of universal human rights with strong claims to public recognition. The universality of the right to self-determination is not doubted and appears to support ethnic self-consciousness. Moreover, ethnicity is not a characteristic of minorities, but an attribute of any group sharing common cultural characteristics.

The very univeralism of ethnicity, however, tends to level the claims that can be made in terms of uniqueness. If each group is unique, what makes any one claim special? Linking the concept of aboriginality to ethnicity is one way in which ethnonational claims are strengthened. Aboriginality asserts a unique presence and a historical particularity to cultural differences. Canadian First Nations and Australian Aboriginals claim not only prior but original occupation. Quebec's claim is emphasized by the historicity of being a 'founding people.' Both Quebecois nationalists and First Nations spokespersons reject the 'ethnic' label which is identified closely with immigrants of many origins. Ethnicity is used in the Canadian debate as a counter to the claims of exclusivity or priority which are inherent in aboriginal-founding status. In Malaysia, aboriginality is used to lend support and give depth to the Malayan assertions of their ethnonationalism as state culture. In the Soviet Union, the ethnonationalism of the major ethnic groups overshadowed the northern peoples who might have used aboriginality to make claims against the state. In 1991 the Soviet Union collapsed and given subsequent events such claims would not have had any political space in which to be heard. In Africa, aboriginality is a value of politics used against Asian and European outsiders. After independence, however, it is a relatively minor question in Kenya and unimportant in Nigeria. Despite many historical accounts of migration and settlement it is not a major issue, perhaps because it was associated during the colonial period with intensified solidarity in opposition to white officials and settlers and this symbolism has not diminished.

Connor (1973: 3) suggested that when the definition of 'nation' was attached to the idea of 'the people' ethnonational claims gained legitimacy. The language of popular self-determination equates these claims with the sovereignty of the encompassing state. The exlcusive sovereignty of the state is questioned in ethnonational claims made by First Nations peoples through the assertion that they are equally 'nations.' This claim which is based on precedent, treaties with the Crown, and autonomy prior to colonial intrusions, and summarized by the term 'aboriginality,' is also a claim for equality. The demand for the right to negotiate 'nation' to 'nation' is important in this rhetoric. Native claims question the basis of justification for sovereignty of the Canadian state. The Innu of Labrador are an example of such radical ethnonational ideology (see paper by Tanner). Where a large number of ethnic groups suggest a clearer threat to the state, in the form of structural change and in terms of lost population, ethnonationalist claims open more decisively the question of the legitimacy of the existing state.

Quebec, as the nation of Canada's francophones, makes similar claims, exept that cultural and linguistic survival in North America is the central concern necessitating self-determination.[1] Political liberty vs. oppression from the centre are not part of the Quebec nationalist rhetoric. The complexity of language issues in Canada, including bilingualism, minorities within Quebec, and the structure of the Canadian federal state have put Quebec at the centre of Canadian constitutional politics for many years. The Quebec case for self-determination has been strengthened by representing itself as a 'nation' seeking autonomy. The language of its claims, in particular, the phrase 'a distinct society' has enriched the vocabulary of Canadian cultural rights. Ironically, this language has worked to undermine Quebec's claim to uniqueness. First Nations and other provinces now argue for their own distinctiveness as if this was a decisively potent political attribute. Thus, while having the strongest claim in its country to self-determination and the warmest reception by any central government of any case considered in these papers, Quebec's success has enriched First Nations claims by creating language that makes a special and universal moral appeal.

Opposition to self-determination is often argued in terms of 'sovereignty,' a term which evokes absoluteness. Its meaning is very strong and attempts to intensify it as 'full sovereignty' seem irrelevant. The use of other modifiers such as partial, shared, or limited, it is argued, makes the term meaningless. Sovereignty suggests the indivisible quality of a nation, which if reduced in any way weakens it. In discussions of self-determination, the universality of the ideal is accepted, but the perceived threat to sovereignty is a major sticking point. The threat to the political sovereignty of the state is often placed in opposition to the claim to self-determination. The question becomes not whether pluralism can be accommodated, but whether the country can accept secession, or separation.

The responses of political leaders to ethnonational aspirations often stifle the aspiration for self-determination. This situation is seen most clearly with regard to territorial conflicts. In Canada, sovereignty for Quebec is a real possibility and for First Nations a provocative point of debate. The state's vigilance to ensure independence from other states can easily be transferred to domestic politics, confusing this aspect of sovereignty with claims of absolute sovereignty in internal affairs and viewing ethnonational politics as the equivalent to external attack. The limits of and the qualified nature of sovereignty in external affairs are rarely appreciated. Even in deep and apparently intractable conflicts, e.g., Israel and its neighbours, suggestions are being made of less than full sovereignty to achieve peace. Negotiations on issues of common interest, e.g., border security and water-sharing, have also been ongoing between Israel and Jordan. Sovereignty, in the sense of the right of a state to manage its own internal affairs, has also been challenged by the international involvement of governments and independent bodies in issues which are of broad human concern, most notably the environment and human rights.

Sovereignty may be viewed as a concept best reserved for the conditional assertion that all governments may face conditions of emergency in which normal constitutional rules have to be set aside if the state is to survive (Crick 1968: 81). For all the countries discussed in this volume, politics is partly a matter of ethnic conciliation. Declarations of emergency may be seen as attempts to push ethnonational political issues out of the realm of politics into the realm of sovereignty, to turn them into a crisis. The strongest ethnonational claims, those for secession, may be seen as threats to sovereignty, but this necessitates a view of the state as absolute and of politics as a continuing emergency. The autonomy and independence evoked by the term 'sovereignty,' however, are implied in First Nations claims in Canada, and explicit in those of Quebec. The language of change and demands for recognition are forced into the restricted discourse of sovereignty and nationalism, since without such strong language these claims are too easily deflected or dismissed outright. The lack of creative solutions in the simplistic idea of state sovereignty constricts the discourse of ethnopolitics.

Ironically, the defense of sovereignty, in order to suppress ethnonational or ethnocultural issues, leads not to strengthening the state, but to questioning its legitimacy. The expression of such aspirations, viewed as 'ethnically inspired dissonance,' is often perceived as a threat to the integrity of the state (Connor 1973: 2). Ethnonational claims, as Connor points out, derive their persuasiveness from the same ideal of national self-determination that led to the formation of many present-day states, especially those who secured their independence from colonial empires. Kenya and Nigeria, which have had to confront their colonial past, have channelled ethnonational aspirations into a common cause – the nation.

The term 'ethnonational' itself has been questioned because of the limits it imposes on discussion and conceptualization of solutions. Since it links ethnicity and nation, 'ethnonational' may be seen to overemphasize the nation as the goal and exclusive form for ethnic aspirations of autonomy. It has been suggested that the term 'ethnocultural,' as it is used by Tanner, might encourage the creation of political forms other than the nation-state as possibilities for the protection of culture and language. 'Ethnocultural' does not have the impact and definitiveness that the term 'nation' carries. Cultural autonomy might move discussion away from such inflammatory issues as sovereignty and secession and toward areas of compromise and negotiation in politics and culture.

THE STATE AND ETHNONATIONALISM

In legitimizing a politics based on ethnic identity, the language of ethnonationalism focuses attention on the state. Aspirations to sovereignty and secession from the state are the central questions in the ethnonational debate. Ethnonational claims are often perceived as self-evident, denying any challenge or opposition and conceiving of self-determination as a purely internal process. If the central role of the state is recognized, as in Connor's view, it is seen as a neutral, rational arbiter confronted with the problems created by the emotional politics of ethnonationalism. It is clear from these papers, however, that the state is a major factor in creating, defining, understanding, and explaining ethnonationalism.

The constitutive role and the pervasive power of the state in influencing the daily life and politics of its cultural communities are acknowledged. The state is seen as defining the political space in which ethnonational claims are made. The way in which national culture is institutionalized is vital in determining whether that space is open or closed to pluralism. The particular state's policy toward pluralism, whether it sets the stage for secession, or whether it provides an arena in which cultural plurality is supported and contained, is discussed in some way in each paper. Weaver, Asch, Macklem, Nagata, Abwunza, and Levin deal directly with the state and its agencies as organizing ethnonational issues. In the papers by Tremblay and Tanner the state is the object against which ethnonational claims are made. In the case of Quebec, it is opposition of one state (Quebec) to another state (Canada).

With the state as the model of government and the association of states and the principles of preservation of the integrity of states the basis of international relations, it is very difficult to see alternatives that are more accommodating to ethnonational aspirations. Quebec and the Innu found polarizations of language and declarations of separation from the existing state the only satisfying alternatives. Quebec's struggle for greater autonomy and sovereignty and the Innu campaign for recognition were extreme cases.

The state has a deliberate proactive role in defining and mediating the issues of pluralism through the constitutions and legal systems. In this role, the state and its agencies recognize the claims of and bestow legal standing on ethnic groups. By allowing a group to make a claim, the state recognizes a relationship and confers on cultural difference a legitimacy that can be achieved in no other way. In Canada and Australia this preliminary form of recognition is well established. In Malaysia, Kenya, and Nigeria, ethnic group claims are not recognized legally, although they are central to constitutional debate and government practice. One problem raised by Macklem and Asch is how to open constitutions that are formed in legal systems that conceive of their descent in a lineal way from a specific and well-articulated legal tradition to new plural conepts. Weaver shows how the agencies of government can direct and distort the process of negotiation, in effect manipulating ethnonational politics to change the form of the aboriginal political community, by encouraging some groups and undermining the authority and effectiveness of others.

The papers by Tanner, Nagata, Abwunza, and Levin draw their second main theme from Connor, in the idea that the origins of ethnonationalism must be discovered, not simply by noting ethnic identity but also by examining how and in what form a people matches identity to a conception of popular sovereignty. These cases represent a wide range of solutions in an historical perspective, from secession to identification of ethnic expression with national goals.

They illustrate how the state, the political space, and the scale of groups create forms of ethnonational expression and also how the state limits its own capacity to satisfy and contain ethnonational aspirations. The emphasis in these papers is on the historical context of the ethnonational claims in the countries in question rather than on the deliberate negotiations on specific issues.

The Innu of Labrador discussed in Tanner's paper have developed a self-identity that is in opposition to 'white' culture. This study gives detail and depth to the constitutional issues raised by Asch and Macklem. Having recently become a sedentary people, and in the process of losing their autonomy, the Innu have developed an indigenous radical ethnonationalist ideology in opposition to the Canadian government, NATO, and industrial developers. Their strategy has been consonant with indigenous political culture and at the same time effective in attracting national and international attention.

The papers on Malaysia, Kenya, and Nigeria demonstrate how federations that have been inescapably plural in culture as colonial states and since independence offer cases in which ethnonational claims and programs have been incorporated into the understandings of the national political culture. All three states were formed as British colonies by merging, through conquest, disparate polities and cultures. Colonial-era governance established a model of a distant, foreign, and racially distinct, but mediating central government, which has been difficult to perpetuate since independence. A romanticized view of the colonial period has converted the distance, ignorance, and arbitrariness of the colonial rulers into disinterestedness and impartiality. Thirty or more years after independence, each of these states has developed policies and institutions which explicitly recognize their cultural plurality. Malaysia has been faced with the central conflict between Malays and Chinese. The first step to resolution of this conflict was the separation of Malaya into Malaysia and Singapore, creating states with majorities. Since this separation the question of the majority Malay ethnonational project has been a central issue in Malaysian politics.

The Malaysian case brings into strongest light the use of the national constitution to promote the ethnicity of the majority as the national culture. The Malays, barely a majority, have been struggling to create and strengthen what they have called an indigenous culture. The attempt to identify Malays with *orang alsi*, the 'original' peoples of the Malay peninsula and the identification of Malaysian identity with Islam has created a fascinating and complex set of criteria and discriminations. This may be seen as an attempt to identify one ethnic group whose cultural transition has a historically very specific aspect – Islam – with aboriginality. It appears to be a somewhat contradictory and contrived effort to create a system which encourages Malayness, and which potentially embraces all residents, but which in practice limits access to that cultural status. The Malaysian case illustrates the manipulative efforts necessary to create a history of indigenousness and the complexity of trying to merge criteria such as faith in a world religion with local aboriginality. In promoting Malaysian culture and identifying it with Islam the Malaysian state has highlighted contradictions between international notions of religious community and local policies of affirmative action and particularism.

Kenya and Nigeria illustrate separate African solutions to ethnonational questions. Kenya has developed an ideology of national integration that embraces all ethnic groups as constituents. Fulfilment of goals, national and ethnic, are argued to be interdependent and not in conflict. As Abwunza shows, the ideology of national integration does not suppress the awareness of ethnic differences, but rather channels ethnonational claims into a self-conscious ideology of nation-building.

The federal system of Nigeria has created a different experience of ethnonational claims. The federation was built on a triangle of ethnic groups, the Igbo, the Yoruba, and Hausa–Fulani, each at the core of a region. The shifting alliances between the Northern Region Hausa–Fulani and one of the Eastern Region Igbo and Western Region Yoruba dominated and crippled Nigerian democratic politics in the First Republic from independence in 1960 to the first military coup in 1966. Politics, rhetoric, and policy centred on these regional-cum-ethnic oppositions. It came to appear that Nigeria had only three ethnic groups, when in fact, more than 40 per cent of Nigerians identified with none of these three. Regional names – the three directions – came to be synonymous for the three ethnic names. The inevitable polarization of Nigerian politics led to the great ethnonational crisis in Nigerian politics, the Biafran Secession, or the Nigerian Civil War, of 1967 to 1970. The story of Nigerian constitutional reorganization is one of accommodating ethnic aspirations and reducing dominance of the larger ethnic groups. Its subtext is the important influence that institutional forms, the jurisdictional structures of government, have in shaping ethnic consciousness.

The contribution by Tremblay on Quebec concerns the preliminaries to secession. Quebec's case for secession is more cultural than political.

An underlying theme of these papers is that the use of compromise, negotiation, and coexistence to create cultural autonomy within existing states is preferable to secession. Constitutional change is the form suggested by Macklem and Asch. Cultural diversity has had explicit recognition in policy and structure and has thus channelled and calmed explosive forces in the cases presented by Abwunza, Levin, and Nagata. Polarized positions, however, seem necessary in order to articulate self-definition and provoke recognition and lead from there to discussions of compromise. In Canada, some leaders in the Assembly of First Nations have entertained the idea of separation, but the 'absolute sovereigntists' are said to be a minority (*Globe and Mail*, 6 June 1991). Armed confrontations between First Nations groups and authorities have focused public attention on the slow pace of negotiations in a number of areas such as land claims, discussions on self-government, and logging and hunting rights. In Labrador, the Innu became more radical in their politics through opposition to NATO training missions overflying their territory (Tanner). It remains to be seen whether a public discussion of the polarized opposition of sovereigntist and independentist claims will lead to political action directed to conciliatory solutions. In cases of proportionately large ethnic groups and those which can claim a territory based on existing jurisdictional boundaries, e.g., Quebec, secession is a practical possibility. Where ethnic or aboriginal groups are small and dispersed, e.g., First Nations in Canada and aboriginals in Australia, such solutions for autonomy are more difficult to plan. One possibility, argued by Asch and Macklem, is for nations to open their cultural self-conception to plural forms, creating opportunities for cultural autonomy within states, perhaps by 'sharing sovereignty' in certain areas of jurisdiction.

Loosening the strictures of ethnopolitical language is a first step in perceiving the demands and claims for recognition as something other than confrontation with the state. One example of this broadening is the generalization of the term 'ethnicity.' The making of constitutions and the recognition of aboriginal concerns in law is another important dimension in deliberate political creation. In the Canadian example discussed by Asch and Macklem, the changes require overcoming historical bias that privileges British and French law over aboriginal ideas of justice and rights, and engaging in a deliberate process of rectifying the exclusion of Canada's original peoples from its constitution. Constitutions themselves, however, are not guarantees of inclusion and openness to cultural diversity.

Solutions to ethnonationalist aspirations require new notions of the state that do not depend on a national culture. It is not always obvious that the cultural content is embedded in patterns of interactions, symbols of trust, and forms of rhetoric, in particular because it is common for the state to see itself as neutral and rational, not as a culturally driven set of institutions. This neutral stance is used by the Canadian state in regard to aboriginal claims, but in regard to Quebec's claim it conflicts with Canada's image as bilingual and bicultural. The Malaysian case is of a strong national culture asserting itself through a blending of aboriginality, Islam, and Malay culture as a vehicle for nation-building. The African cases, Kenya and Nigeria, suggest a solution that is most incorporative of all the examples here: diverse cultures are explicitly recognized and diversity and cultural difference are understood as based in tradition and are treated as an aspect of nationalism. It is clear that the state, if accommodating, if not tied to a narrow nationalism, may open a society to cultural diversity.

The alternative to accommodation – suppressing cultural expression – is counterproductive as it leads to intensification of a sense of victimization and separateness. It is equally damaging to allow recognition of ethnicity to be confining of individuals as many examples from Africa, Europe, and Asia would demonstrate. The manipulation of ethnopolitical issues is possible, but it is but a version of suppression and the evidence from many countries indicates that the issues do not disappear. The difficult challenge to governments is to extend their cultural definition of citizenship. For most states this requires reassessment of their histories and likely raises painful issues of 'redress' for past events. Historical accounting is central to most issues in which aboriginality is the basis of the ethnopolitics. In Africa, however, some of these issues have been displaced because of the 'oppositions' inherent in the colonial structure of the states. Aboriginality, for example, has been largely eliminated from the historical dimension of ethnic politics because European colonialism created an era in which unity of African peoples was forged out of common subservience and common struggle for independence. Differences that might have arisen out of their precolonial relationships were suppressed.

For Canada, recognition of aboriginality as a basis for legitimate political participation in the constitutional debate and the creation of parallel or autonomous legal systems will not only acknowledge claims made to remedy historical disenfranchisement, dislocation, and exploitation, but also recognize symbolically and constitutionally that aboriginality bestows rights on certain groups and to place this recognition at the centre of national self-conception. Despite public statements of good faith, however, aboriginal claims have met with resistance. Weaver shows how, in Australia, aboriginal organizations have been manipulated and pitted against one another. Macklem contends that the Canadian legal system has defined aboriginal identity in such a way as to reduce native claims to sovereignty and restrict rights over land. Asch further argues that full participation of indigenous peoples depends on constitutional change which would also lead to the renewal of Canadian confederation.

It is almost self-evident to say today that nations are invented. The judgments attached to this view range from distinct hostility to enthusiastic acceptance, but the truth in the idea that old and new nationalism change and depend on imagination and creativity has been established. The Canadian constitutional revisions and the juggling of state and local government boundaries in Nigeria are forms of invention.

The discussion of ethnonationalism in this collection has focused on issues of sovereignty, aspirations of self-determination, and expressions of ethnic identity. The similarities of the claims and language do not, however, obscure the variation in the forms and circumstances in each case. The comparative approach characteristic of anthropology has facilitated the analysis of how states and their majority and minority cultures seek political expression. A failure to allow the expression of cultural diversity stifles the process of national reinvention and creates fatal rigidity of the state, as in pre–Civil War Nigeria. Where a state is open to accommodation and incorporation of these forms of political expression, it may temper extreme ethnonational responses and contribute to its own reinvention and renewal. We can agree, therefore, with Connor that the power of the idea of self-determination of nations is far from spent. This discussion reveals the benefits of recognizing its legitimacy.

NOTES

1 One of the contested points in Quebec's claims to self-determination is whether Quebec speaks for Canadian francophones, or for all residents of Quebec. Francophone communities outside Quebec, in Ontario, the

Western Provinces, as well as Acadians in New Brunswick, Nova Scotia, and Prince Edward Island often complain that their language rights are unprotected in Canadian constitutional negotiations, which have been in process since the 1970s more or less continuously until the present time.

REFERENCES

Anderson, Benedict. 1991. *Imagined Communities: Reflections on the Origin and Spread of Nationalism*, 2nd ed. London: Verso

Connor, Walker. 1973. 'The politics of ethnonationalism.' *Journal of International Affairs* 27(1): 1–21

Crick, Bernard. 1968. 'Sovereignty.' *International Encylopedia of the Social Sciences* 15: 77–82

Glazer, Nathan and Daniel P. Moynihan (eds.). 1975. *Ethnicity: Theory and Experience*. Cambridge: Harvard University Press

Contributors

Judith M. Abwunza — Department of Anthropology, University of Western Ontario, London, Ontario

Michael Asch — Department of Anthropology, University of Alberta, Edmonton, Alberta

Michael D. Levin — Department of Anthropology, University of Toronto, Toronto, Ontario

Patrick Macklem — Faculty of Law, University of Toronto, Toronto, Ontario

Judith Nagata — Department of Anthropology, York University, Downsview, Ontario

Adrian Tanner — Department of Anthropology, Memorial University, St John's, Newfoundland

Marc-Adélard Tremblay — Department of Anthropology, Laval Unversity, Quebec City, Quebec

Sally Weaver — Department of Anthropology, University of Waterloo, Waterloo, Ontario